How to stand up to
Workplace Bullying
And take on an
Unjust Employer

Published by Marfa House
Copyright 2016 Sumi Mukherjee

Marfa House
Marfa, Texas

Marfa House

Marfa, Texas

How to Stand up to Workplace Bullying and Take on an Unjust Employer

Published by Marfa House

Copyright 2016 by Sumi Mukherjee
1st Edition

ISBN: 978-1-946072-24-5

ALSO BY SUMI MUKHERJEE:

A life interrupted: The Story Of My Battle With Bullying And Obsessive Compulsive Disorder

Father Figure: My Mission To Prevent Child Sexual Abuse

Table of Contents

Acknowledgements

First and foremost - on a personal level - I would like to thank my family and friends whose presence over the years has helped me to reach my potential and to now try to help others.

I would also like to thank a number of my coworkers over the years who have supported me in my battle against workplace bullying. Their encouragement and sincere advice have played a key role in my decision to stand up to bullying in the workplace and to write this book that will help both employees and employers around the country to maintain a safe work environment that promotes overall success for everyone involved.

I would also like to thank Sonia Miller-Van Oort, Attorney & Founder at Sapientia Law Group in Minneapolis, MN, for her legal support of this book.

Dedicated to...

This book is dedicated to all people around the world who believe that a safe and fair workplace is critical for professional success for everyone and are working sincerely to achieve the goal of maintaining a harmonious workplace.

How to Stand up to Workplace Bulling
And Take on an Unjust Employer

During my senior year of high, I was the student voted most likely to disrupt and expose ongoing corruption within an established organization. **–Sumi Mukherjee**

Introduction

The following account is based on a true story. Besides using my own real name; I have created pseudonyms, fictitious names, for all the other characters involved to protect their identities. I have also chosen not to name the locations in which these real-life events took place for the very same reason.

This book was written, first and foremost, for the vulnerable children whom I had the pleasure of working with over the years. It was written for their parents as well, who made the courageous decision to reach out and ask the system for help in preventing child abuse and neglect.

This book was written for every legally mandated reporter employed in the United States. Although I'm not a lawyer or giving legal advice, I have written this book to give additional perspective and to support you in your performance of your job duties as you look out for the well-being of children you oversee. I hope that my story will give you courage to meet your responsibilities, without fear of retaliation from your employers.

This book is also for anyone who has been, or is currently being treated unjustly at their place of employment and simply does not know how to obtain relief. Your situation may have you convinced there's nothing you can do to change it; at least that's what your arrogant bully employer would love for you to believe. In this revealing book, I will share my most unique employment experiences, challenging an employer's vain perspective and show you how an ordinary person CAN and SHOULD stand up for their rights at the workplace!

It was Thursday, May 6, 1976 at the Foothills Hospital in Calgary, Alberta, Canada. The time was about 2:24 p.m. Although most people do not remember a whole lot about the day they were born; I have always been able to vividly recall my very first, precious moments as a tiny little person on this earth. After my mother had given birth to me, the doctor carefully placed me in the room where all newborns are put for observation. I remember being in complete awe of the amazingly complex, beautiful new world around me. As I lay there feeling safe and content; I felt assured that this was the first day of what would surely be a very long, prosperous and wonderful life for me.

Then before I knew it, I heard a barely audible snickering coming from the nearby cribs. To my utter shock and dismay, other newborn babies in the room were laughing and pointing at me. "Oh look, there's an ugly, brown, Indian baby!" one of them said. "Yeah, and he has such a ridiculous name too!" added another. Before long all the babies in the observation room were making fun of me together, calling me brown, different-looking, a foreigner, an outsider, ugly, shit-colored and overly hairy. As if this weren't traumatic enough, soon they were all spitting out their pacifiers and throwing them at me as well. The boy babies said they would never want to be friends with such an ugly, brown, Indian child; and the girl babies said they would never even consider dating such an ugly, brown, Indian man later on in their teenage years or adulthood. I was utterly appalled and devastated. As I looked around the room, suddenly overwhelmed with feelings of self-consciousness and embarrassment, little did I realize that this incident was merely a preview of what the next couple decades of my lifetime would bring.

In fact, it would only be after three and a half decades wrought with bullying, racial discrimination and mental illness that I would finally become an expert in understanding how to deal with and defeat the bullies living among us; especially in regards to dealing with bully employers at our places of work.

As a result, I hope that you can now benefit significantly from what I have learned in my life!

Chapter One
Don't Sue Me, Sumi

"Bullies are just friends who don't realize how special you are yet!"
**Statement made by character Angie Lopez to her grade school
age son, Max, during an episode of the TV sitcom George Lopez.**

Alright now, I must admit in all fairness that the introduction you
just read may not be 100 percent on point with its accuracy
regarding what occurred on the day that I was born. However, at
thirty-five years of age in 2011, I had often felt over my lifetime as
though I was indeed born to be bullied. Being the firstborn child
of immigrant parents from India and being raised in Midwestern
America, I grew up during the 1980s and '90s in an
overwhelmingly white, conservative state. In the fall of 1981, at
the age of five; I began attending Kindergarten in a quiet, peaceful
town; which was a suburb of the nearby metropolis.

Literally from Kindergarten all the way through 9th grade, I was
bullied relentlessly by my peers on a regular basis. This ongoing
harassment was worst during elementary and middle school.
Though the situation greatly improved by the later years of high
school; I was generally still treated as an outcast who didn't fit in.
There were a handful of reasons as to why this awful predicament
became my fate. The reasons included my being a very nice kid,
my extreme sensitivity to harassment by peers and my burning
desire to seek revenge against those who had treated me badly.

By far, the clearest reasons for my problems were my highly
unusual name and physical appearance. At the three different

schools I attended in my hometown from grades K-12, I was one of the very few students who was neither white nor black; and furthermore, I truly stood out as one of the very, very precious few whose parents were immigrants from India and had grown up on the opposite end of the planet.

You can sure bet that the people around me noticed. Beginning in Kindergarten, I was harassed on a regular basis by a group of sixth graders who rode on the same bus as I did. I remember feeling petrified of them and having nightmares about them coming after me. It took several trips to the principal's office and still the harassment would not stop. "This is Sumi's problem and it's HIS responsibility to resolve it!" the hard-ass principal scolded my parents. Only after other young children reported the same group of sixth graders to the principal, did the school finally take any action toward correcting this awful behavior.

After Kindergarten, I was primarily picked on by my own grade level peers, along with kids who were directly one grade above and below me. Unlike with the group of sixth graders from kindergarten, my same age peers openly shared their motivation in choosing to single me out. In short there were many degrading remarks directed to me throughout the years about my ethnicity; country of origin; brown skin complexion and dark-colored, black hair. Even while I grew up viewing myself as being no different from any other human being around me, many children had a very different point of view on that particular subject. And so did some of the faculty, as I remember one instance in high school when my grade level principal tactlessly said to me in a conversation, "Oh Sumi, there's nobody else in this entire school that looks *anything* like you!"

Besides my physical appearance, one can break down my peers' main triggers for harassing me into three separate features which were unique just to me and me only; these features being My First Name, My Middle Name and My Last Name.

How to Stand up to Workplace Bulling
And Take on an Unjust Employer

Sumit Sagar Mukherjee. Ah yes, that is my first, middle and last name which I can now say out loud with feelings of pride, tragically unlike when I was growing up as a child. All throughout school, a large number of my peers taunted me continuously relating to the three parts of my full name. But more than anything else, the kids absolutely loved to tease me most about my first name. Though my full first name is 'Sumit', I had always merely gone by 'Sumi' from the time I was very young.

In retrospect, this may not have been such a great idea, as I found myself always hearing what became the same old sickening, ever so cleverly stated one liner; "Don't sue me... Sumi!" Ah yes, if I had a dollar for every time I've heard that brilliant line quoted back to me blended in with stupid giggles and laughter, I would never have to work another day in my life. Ultimately, such relentless harassment on a regular basis, including people yelling and singing my name in the hallways, triggered the onset of an extremely crippling anxiety disorder in my mid-teens. This onset occurred during my high school years, ironically just as the long-term harassment from my peers was finally beginning to decline. Only at age thirty-five, after suffering indescribably for more than half my life, had I *finally* learned how to control my once incapacitating symptoms and resume a fulfilling existence. For more information on my triumph over adversity, please see my earlier book titled "A Life Interrupted: The Story Of My Battle With Bullying And Obsessive-Compulsive Disorder."

Still tragically, I continued to find bullying and differential treatment in my post high school life as well. It came in the forms of racial discrimination in relation to dating girls, as well as problems at various places of employment. At my first job working at a local hotel, I encountered prejudice from my general manager's wife, specifically over my unusual appearance and ethnic background. During my second job working at a hotel front desk, I found myself being singled out for ridicule by my condescending supervisor. This treatment was even noticeable by our customers, one of whom I recall wrote the following remarks about it on a comment card to our hotel management: "The man at the desk was being condescending toward the young man who was helping us check in." Much like during my days in grade school, I had to seek help from higher authority figures to finally get this harassment to stop. Even after it did, I then found myself being bullied even more harshly by the front office department manager! Being only 19 years of age and extremely inexperienced, I simply opted to leave this negative environment and quit that job without giving two weeks' notice. Looking back on it now, I realize that I could have taken a different approach in asserting my rights with my employer.

However, it would be several more years before such meaningful revelations would come my way through age and experience. As it turned out, it would be through more painful experience in which I would find myself becoming a victim yet again.

Still I never dreamed for a moment that the longstanding, comedic prediction repeatedly made by my peers throughout school would ever possibly come true; that I would find myself in a position where I felt I would actually need to sue someone.

BULLIES OF THE WORLD BEWARE! Coincidence or Karma? You read it and decide.

In June 2000, at the age of 24, I looked up and confronted my absolute worst childhood bully of all time, whom I will call Michael Beckert. In fact, it was the mental image of Michael's smirking face that assumed a leading role in determining the horrendous ways in which my Obsessive-Compulsive Disorder (OCD) symptoms played out. You can read more about Michael Beckert in chapter ten of my first book, "A Life Interrupted: The Story Of My Battle With Bullying And Obsessive-Compulsive Disorder".

When I confronted him in June 2000, Michael appeared to be a shell of the former awful jerk who had tormented me without mercy. Little did I know at the time that Michael had suffered an onset of Schizo-Affective Disorder four years earlier, at the age of 19. The main school bully who contributed most to my developing a severe mental illness, had incredibly suffered an even worse mental illness in his own life!

While randomly surfing the net on Google a decade later in June 2010, I was stunned to suddenly come upon Michael's obituary and learn that Michael had killed himself in 2008 at the age of 31. That's right. A dozen years of schizophrenia had hounded him into an early grave. I found it quite ironic that in the five years preceding my proper OCD diagnosis in 1997, I myself had lived under the constant fear that perhaps I, too, was schizophrenic!

Most ironic of all is the fact that Michael's funeral took place at a church which was located on a street with the name of 'Summit Ave', which is almost exactly the same spelling as my full first name, Sumit. Either way, it is the name that Michael Beckert had mocked so thoroughly during his shortened life.

Chapter Two

Getting Screwed in Someone Else's Affair

"Warning: Discussing personal matters with coworkers can be hazardous to your employment."

In the years following my OCD diagnosis in March 1997, I worked hard toward my recovery and to take back control of my life. Along with some periods of time when I was unable to work, I soon found myself taking college courses and/or working at different hotels. Upon beginning a new hotel job in October 2003, I was finally at a point where I could live life again, and relish some fun and good times.

As a result, I approached this front desk job in a somewhat immature and carefree manner. Rather than being serious or focused at giving my best, I instead became a popular jokester and the life of the party at work. For the first time in my entire life, I had seemingly achieved a measure of acceptance among my peers. In fact, it was through hanging out with a coworker socially, outside of our place of employment, that my job would soon become jeopardized in a way I could not have imagined.

The day was April 1, 2004, and I remember this primarily because; ironically, it had been April Fools' Day. As it turned out, I would end up playing the fool. During my shift at work, a female colleague asked me if I wanted to get together after our shift and hang out. Upon doing so that evening, my colleague and I ended up having a few beers back at my house. It was during this beer drinking, however, that my colleague went on to disclose to me that she had been having a romantic affair with our front office supervisor! This was quite a shock for me to hear, as I had never suspected that anything had been occurring between these two particular individuals. Over the next several hours, until 5 a.m. the following morning; my colleague told me all the intimate details about this secret, months-long relationship. These revealing disclosures included information about how she and the supervisor had been intimate in the hotel parking lot, in the service elevator and even in the office of our feared department boss!

In the days that followed, I simply couldn't keep this juicy bombshell of a story to myself. Although my colleague had asked me not to tell anybody about this, I informed my two closest friends among the front office staff who I thought I could trust. While my best buddy kept these details under wraps, the second colleague whom I had confided to went on to tell several other people about this. Eventually when the story went public among the employees, my colleague who had talked then lied to our bosses saying that *I was the one* who had spread it. While I readily admitted to telling the two individuals with whom I had spoken in private, I insisted that I had not told all the others who had later found out about this.

Regardless of the truth in my declarations, my managers did not believe me. This was somewhat because of the fact that over the past six months of my employment at this hotel, my reputation as a carefree jokester had served to tarnish my professional image. Indeed, I had been guilty of committing numerous minor pranks and of goading others into such behavior as well. The fact that I was telling the truth about this became easy to overlook.

In the days that followed, I was suspended from work and investigated by the hotel's Human Resources Manager. Although the manager attempted to listen to all different sides of this puzzling story; she went on to conclude, improperly, that I was indeed the one who had told several other people about this.

Finally, on Wednesday, April 14, 2004, I was fired from my job at the hotel for allegedly spreading these rumors; which the hotel claimed amounted to sexual harassment. I found it especially interesting that even in deciding to terminate my employment over this matter, the hotel's HR Manager verbally conceded to me that; "We may never know exactly what all occurred in this situation." Outraged that I had not been believed and was treated so unjustly, I promised the HR Manager that this 'matter' was far from concluded.

Following my termination and with the full support of my parents, I began to search for a lawyer. Fortunately, this quest was made much easier by the fact that my best buddy and coworker already knew of a very good one. In fact, my friend had previously used the services of this particular attorney when he had issues of his own with the management of our hotel. Therefore, I had been saved, at least this time around, from the efforts it would take to go out and find an attorney.

Upon contacting the recommended lawyer and setting up an appointment, my dad and I met with the gentleman in the weeks after my termination. This guy was a calm, soft spoken young man who had a clear recollection of the earlier work he had done for my best friend and colleague. He also remembered his prior experience working with this hotel's attorney, and it didn't take long for us to brief him about my new situation. Along with firmly validating our belief that I was indeed treated unfairly, this lawyer agreed to take on my case and challenge my termination. I made it clear that my goal was to simply have my termination reversed, specifically so that I would not have to possibly tell new employers that I had been fired. I took great pride in the fact that I had never been fired before, and was certainly committed to wanting to keep my employment record that way. Along with this primary motivation, I was also driven by the need to truly show the hotel that I HAD been telling the truth. After all, why would anybody hire a costly attorney if they knew they had been in the wrong?

Over the following weeks and months, my lawyer communicated several times with the hotel's attorney. Most notably during this period, I was gratified to learn that the hotel's HR Manager had sounded "very scared and nervous" in a voice message that she had left in response to my lawyer's first phone call. But aside from this one little bright spot, it would be quite a while before any substantial progress would be made in my case.

Finally, after four long months of patiently waiting, a form of justice would eventually come my way. It arrived as a copy of a letter from the hotel's attorney to my lawyer, which was dated Monday, August 9, 2004. Although firmly refusing to acknowledge any notion of wrongdoing on the hotel's behalf, the letter said the hotel was willing to make the following 'generous' offer to me, simply for the purpose of "limiting its ongoing legal expense related to this matter." The letter then went on to make the offer mentioned below:

The hotel is agreeable to the following terms:

- *the hotel is agreeable to extending Mr. Mukherjee's date of termination to September 30th 2004;*

- *the hotel would designate Mr. Mukherjee's termination as "voluntary" and take such actions as are necessary to update his personnel file to reflect this;*

- *the hotel would agree to remove the disciplinary action form dated April 14th 2004, from Mr. Mukherjee's file as requested;*

- *the hotel will respond to future employment inquiries in accordance with its established policy of simply confirming position and dates of employment; and*

- *the hotel agrees to pay two weeks' severance to Mr. Mukherjee.*

While this offer was certainly not the best I could have expected, or hoped for, it provided me the victory and validation that I needed to move on with my life. Most gratifying of all, was the fact that my disciplinary papers would be shredded and my departure would be termed as 'voluntary' to future employers.

But perhaps even more beneficial, were the life lessons I learned from this bizarre workplace situation. I learned how one must guard and limit conversations with their coworkers, especially concerning personal and sensitive subject matter that can be labeled as gossip and/or sexual harassment. I also realized that, although I had indeed been treated unfairly, I had not put forth my best effort in establishing myself as a credible employee. All the good jokes, pranks and camaraderie; while they made me a popular guy, had adversely affected my image in the eyes of the people in charge. Such actions had slowly chipped away at my credibility, and made it difficult for my managers to believe that I was telling the truth.

But even in such a poorly handled situation, where I did not keep documentation or excel in personal responsibility, I had learned what can happen when and if an individual is able to stand up for their rights. Had I not hired a lawyer and put some pressure on the hotel, they would not have taken actions to correct their unjust mistake.

Taking life in the workplace seriously was perhaps the greatest lesson I had learned. It also proved to be a lesson which would benefit me should I face such unfairness again.

Chapter Three

From Hospitality World to Child Care

"I left hotels for child care because I felt it was easier to deal with unruly little children than it was to deal with unruly grown adults."

Following my untimely departure from the hospitality world, my life proceeded to go in many different directions. Most negatively, I would end up going off my OCD medications and then suffering a devastating relapse during the remainder of 2004. This major, life consuming setback would eventually lead me to enter a residential treatment program in April 2005, which ultimately helped me to take back control of my life from my OCD.

During this extreme hardship and afterwards, I also began to grow very close to a former coworker at the hotel from where I had departed. Though this lady and I would eventually begin dating many months after we were reintroduced, my connection to her was first cemented through my willingness to personally mentor her deeply troubled nine-year-old son. Although she and I had worked in different departments within the same hotel, we were reintroduced through a mutual friend in the months following my departure.

It was during this reintroduction that I was, for the first time in August 2004, introduced to this lady's young son, whom I will call Peter. Although he was about to turn nine when I met him, little Peter had a rather adult like persona about him. As I got to know both mother and son better, I slowly came to learn just how much trauma Peter had been through during his relatively short time in this world.

Peter, along with his mother, had been physically and verbally abused by his father for years. When the mother had worked overnights at the hotel, the father would force Peter to view pornography in the house with him. Over the years, the father had taken Peter to bars: allowed him to try cigarettes/alcohol; and even held a pillow over Peter's face to control him. Peter had also been beaten by his father, and had witnessed his father beating and abusing his mother. On top of all this, Peter had also been sexually abused on multiple occasions by an older male cousin. Child protective services had investigated claims concerning Peter's mistreatment at the hands of both the father and the male cousin, but for various reasons the legal process did not move further than that in either case. By the time I met Peter, his father had run out on him and his mom, and the couple had gotten a divorce.

Upon meeting, I immediately found Peter to be an unusually fascinating child, and quite a smooth operator as well; especially for a nine-year-old boy. Due to overexposure to adult situations, Peter had a unique ability to converse with grown-ups in a seemingly sophisticated manner. Peter was also very manipulative, strong-willed and highly convincing. He had the demeanor and superficial charm of a natural born salesman, and was someone who frequently appeared to have a specific personal agenda when interacting with others. One example in particular still stands out in my mind. Even though he is clearly Caucasian, young Peter had successfully persuaded several of his second-grade peers at elementary school into believing that the famous black rapper, widely known as 50 Cent, was indeed his biological father!

It should go without saying that Peter had an entertaining personality that would naturally draw people in. Unfortunately,

Peter was also an extremely defiant; unruly; and angry young boy. He had a long history of trouble at school, lying to authority figures and even had a run-in or two with the police. Peter was also incredibly sexualized for his young age, and often behaved/spoke at length in a very graphic sexual manner. When I met Peter in August 2004, his greatest aspiration in life was to someday become a big gangster and to wreak havoc upon the world.

Prior to meeting Peter, I had not had much experience dealing with troubled children. But I had always loved kids, been great with them and hoped to have some of my own one day. Being unemployed and now having all the time in the world, I eventually took it upon myself to become a full-time mentor to Peter. I listened tirelessly to his many troubles, attended all major school/medical/family activities, and worked tremendously hard to bridge the communication gap between mother and son.

As time slowly passed, we began to see amazing changes in Peter's overall behavior and attitude. Many other people picked up on this as well, including some who had previously written Peter off as truly being a lost cause. But I, even out of those in Peter's extended family, was the main one who supported and believed in Peter throughout the most difficult times. In short time, Peter came to consider me a real father figure to him.

The more increasingly positive results we all saw in Peter, the better I felt about my involvement in his life. There was almost no feeling quite as wonderful as having the power to properly raise a child and to help him/her grow and develop in a healthy manner. Eventually, I came into contact with several of Peter's young friends and acquaintances, many of whom had endured difficult upbringings quite similar to his. As a result of slowly mentoring all of these kids, I developed a strong desire to work in a job helping troubled children.

This new major life interest, triggered primarily by my success with Peter, led me into taking college courses in the line of caring for children. Along with attending college, I began to volunteer with agencies which catered to children in trouble. Before long, I found myself volunteering my time at two such prominent child care facilities.

Eventually after many months of dedicated service, one of the two centers awarded me the unexpected high honor of being labeled its "Volunteer of the Year" for 2006. In fact, here is an exact quotation about me from the organization which was proudly displayed on the center's website for the community and public to view:

Sumi Mukherjee has been a child care volunteer for over a year now. In that year, he has logged over 160 hours playing, nurturing and just plain having fun with the children. He is an inspiration to us all with his continually positive attitude and fun spirit. He adores children and they are mad about him. We feel very lucky to have Sumi a part of our volunteer team.

Upon receiving this great recognition in May 2007, I applied for a job right there and was quickly accepted. And so I began my new employment, and this bright new phase of my life, working at the center as a paid employee on May 29, 2007. I naturally loved my new job with the children as expected, and was able to grab a full-time position in early September of that year. Over time, I began to develop a popular persona with the children while employed at the center. I was known to them all affectionately as 'Mr. Sumi,' and they all seemed very excited to have a caring adult male role model around them. Most of the children who stayed at the center did not have fathers in their lives, and some even urged me to date their moms so that I could become their dad! Soon my name became well-known among the parents of these children as well, as they would tell me how their children would look forward to returning to the center just to see their favorite 'Mr. Sumi.'

Unfortunately, this sense of comfort and fulfillment would soon be interrupted by a new round of problems. In retrospect, I suppose these problems were not all that new to me in the big picture. It was the same darn thing that had happened to me throughout school and in my prior work life. Just as I'm beginning to find my own way, a new bully would soon come along....

Chapter Four

Behold the Big Bully Boss Lady

"I always felt as though Hilda Hullickson could have had a rather successful career working as a prison guard within the department of corrections, rather than at a facility where she was placed in charge of society's most vulnerable children."

After all that has occurred over the past several years, it seems strange to recall now how things between child care supervisor, Hilda Hullickson, and I had actually started out on the right foot. In retrospect today, I can summarize my numerous issues with my supervisor at the center in three simple words: HILDA'S HORRIBLE TEMPER.

Even when not agitated, Hilda Hullickson's presence in a room was a difficult thing to ignore. A physically heavyset, large, and imposing woman; Hilda naturally had a commanding presence which followed her wherever she went. In addition to this, she also had a bold personality, loud voice, accompanying body language, and overall demeanor which came across to many as intimidating. This was perhaps true most of all with the children at our center. Regardless of how poorly the children may have been acting out at a given moment, a mere silent stare from Hilda was often enough to quickly redirect their behavior. Hilda served her role as PM shift child care supervisor quite well in this regard; as even the naughtiest, most poorly behaving children would listen to Hilda after they repeatedly refused to follow instructions from anyone else.

However, there would also be numerous occasions when I felt Hilda would cross the line and be excessively harsh, mean, and even abusive toward the children and her staff alike. In fact, Mary Monahan, a fabulous, one of a kind long time shift leader; supervisor; veteran child care provider; and loving grandmother, would appropriately characterize Hilda as being "Harsh toward staff and harsh toward kids." This harshness was likely the result of Hilda's relatively short temper, as she would become red faced and agitated often without much provocation. From the very beginning of Hilda's employment within the organization, Mary and the previous PM shift supervisor had observed behavior from Hilda, toward children, which they both apparently found to be at least 'borderline abusive.' Regardless of their concerns, it never appeared as though much was done by management to redirect Hilda's behavior. In general, Hilda was known as a crabby and grumpy supervisor by most of her regular staff, and her harshness to both staff and children alike was largely taken for granted.

Unfortunately, such 'harsh' treatment by Hilda soon appeared to apply most of all toward me, typically the only male staff person working under her direct supervision. Although Hilda and I had been quite chummy with one another during my days as a child care volunteer, Hilda inexplicably began to direct her aggression toward me in particular once I became an employee. This started shortly after Hilda officially became my supervisor in September 2007, which was also when I acquired a full-time position at the center. At first I merely dismissed such incidents as being isolated occurrences, as Hilda and I had previously gotten along quite well. In fact, Hilda herself gave me a glowing performance review dated October 13, 2007. The review reads exactly as follows, and includes high ratings in nearly all the different, specific areas describing my job performance and interactions with children:

Sumi is always a pleasure to have on afternoons. While on-call, he was very flexible and willing to pick up shifts where ever needed.

Now as full time he is still flexible to switching shifts with others. He appears to genuinely enjoy his time with the kids. He is always interacting well with the children. Sumi is a great role model for the kids.

Sumi is very professional and upholds our mission statement to the fullest. He is very positive when redirecting children; he does well with challenging children using the organization's 'approach to Children/infants.'

Overall, Sumi does a great job. He is a real team player picking up hours and hopefully will enjoy being here as a full-time employee. Thank you, Sumi, for all you do!

Yet with time, it appeared that Hilda's actions spoke a whole lot louder than her kindly written words, and I mean that literally. On one occasion over the next several months, a child assigned to the care of my friendly coworker, Mary Monahan, accidentally dropped some food on the floor in the dining room. While making a list of bathing assignments on the blackboard, Hilda suddenly looked up right at me and then, in front of everyone, bellowed, "SUMI, I KNOW YOU SAW THAT CHILD DROP HER FOOD … NOW YOU GET UP AND GET IT!"

Though stunned at her brazen rudeness, I immediately got up from my chair and went to clean the child's food from the floor, as my supervisor had instructed me to do. Later that same evening, both Mary and another coworker approached me separately and told me that they felt Hilda's outburst was "clearly out of line and very unprofessional." Mary, in particular, further stated to me her honest confusion over why Hilda had singled me out in this instance. "That child who dropped her food was MY responsibility, Sumi, and NOT yours," the gentle Mary commented as a genuine look of concern slowly spread across her face. "I don't understand why Hilda chose to ONLY holler at you." Needless to say, I did not understand it either. However, there would be several other similar instances in the many months that followed. Over time this treatment affected my self-esteem, and brought back PTSD and memories of the relentless bullying from my past. It seemed as though I had yet another 'Michael Beckert' in my life once again.

Regardless, I still felt unsure of what exactly I should do about it. However, there was no uncertainty in my mind when it came to my witnessing Hilda's poor treatment of the children. During the last few days of April 2008, I witnessed a disturbing incident in which Hilda bellowed at a four- year-old child and then shoved the child to the floor during snack time in the dining room. The child happened to fall at my feet where I was seated, as well as at the feet of a brand-new volunteer working her very first shift at our center. Following set procedure as a legally mandated reporter, I went on to write up supervisor Hilda's misconduct and submit my report to Children's Services Manager, Candy Rollins. At first, Candy appeared to take a genuine interest in the matter, and promised that she would get back to me pending her own 'investigation.' However, Candy declined to ever speak to me about this matter again. In the meantime, other coworkers approached me and said they thought it was pretty gutsy of me to actually write up our supervisor. Also, based on the fact that the shoved child had fallen directly at my feet, it would likely not be difficult for Hilda to deduce which staff person had written her up. Incredibly, despite both me and a volunteer being eyewitnesses to this assaultive behavior, Hilda continued to be employed at the center.

The only probable feedback that I did receive, however, came to me in a new job performance review given to me again by Hilda on June 2, 2008, which reads exactly as follows:

Sumi has shown that he is dedicated to the children and really cares for each of them. He seems to enjoy working with the kids. It is a pleasure to see him interact with the children. He is on time

23

for work and doesn't call in. His attendance has proven that he is a dedicated worker. Sumi is friendly and courteous to the volunteers and his peers. He is a valuable asset to the organization.

I would like to see Sumi more willing to answer the door and phone line. This would be a great help in the evenings.

Sumi is a pleasure to have on the afternoon shift and always makes sure that the shift is covered when he needs a day off. He does a wonderful job; he is always helpful to do any task that is asked of him. Thank you, Sumi for your helpfulness and genuine care for all the kids. Thanks for all that you contribute here at the center!

In spite of these positive written words on my review; I also noticed that my ratings had dropped significantly across the board, in several of the different, specific areas describing my job performance and interactions with children. And strangely, there was no further documentation accompanying the ratings to justify or explain why they had dropped; or for that matter, to counsel me on what I could do to improve my supposedly lacking performance. Most concerning of all; was the fact that my rating for the category of "Professional Code of Conduct," had gone down from a 90, which is labeled as 'distinguished;' all the way down to a mere 70, which is labeled as barely meeting the 'minimum' required standard. I wondered if this was a clever message to me from Hilda, in a disguised attempt to warn me that there may be further consequences for me if I chose to write up my supervisor again. Perhaps, I wondered, does 'Professional Code of Conduct' secretly refer to knowing when to keep my mouth shut about my supervisor's mistreatment of children?

As the summer of 2008 progressed, the working relationship between Hilda and me continued to deteriorate. Over time, it appeared to me that Hilda would make a conscious effort to create situations in which the outcome would unfairly result in attempted, if not successful, discipline coming towards me from her. This pattern, along with the frequent harsh, public verbal reprimands, soon became overwhelming for me. Not knowing how to deal with this, I sought professional advice from my friend Connie Cooper, a long-time employee at the other child care facility where I had previously volunteered my time. During the time that I had volunteered my services, Connie had felt I had a natural ability to work superbly well with children and we had therefore remained in contact. Since then I had come to consider Connie to be a mentor to me in the area of caring for children in a professional setting.

Upon speaking with her over the phone, Connie strongly suggested that I begin to meticulously document all the various negative interactions that I was having with Hilda at the workplace. Connie advised that I do so by keeping written record of the specific dates and times when problems occurred, as well as describing exactly what had taken place in each separate instance; including keeping track of who was present, the specific circumstances, and potential witnesses to each incident. Connie further suggested that I do not gossip or discuss these matters with anyone else at the workplace, including my closest friends there. I had learned this lesson the hard way at my last hotel job. Connie also recommended that I bring my issues with Hilda to the attention of our employee union.

As it turned out, the child care facility where Connie was employed had a contract with the same employee union as the center where I was now working. I followed this advice in July 2008 and again in Oct. 2008 to try and constructively resolve the ongoing problems. These efforts consisted of meetings I had with my union representative; Children's Services Manager, Candy Rollins; and our Human Resources Director. I also challenged Hilda's findings in my June 2008 performance review, but management failed to even acknowledge the possibility that I may have experienced retaliation from Hilda for writing her up. While these meetings did seem to calm things down temporarily, it wasn't long before Hilda would start it up all over again. Once again, it looked as though I would continue to be bullied by Hilda, and so would the children at our center.

Keeping accurate documentation/written records of unfair treatment at the workplace; especially that which violates company policies and labor laws, is an excellent way in which to empower yourself against a possibly unjust employer. Simply documenting inappropriate conduct in writing is something that any one of us can easily do, if willing to invest the time and effort. It can also provide the framework for reporting such misconduct to management and beyond as well as strengthening future potential legal claims.

During the summer and fall of 2008, we had a very physically aggressive; exceptionally defiant; and unruly child placed in our care on a regular basis. At bedtime, this child made a habit of intentionally urinating on her mattress and bed sheets, so that staff would have to remake her bed which resulted in the child's bedtime being further delayed. In an effort to defeat this child at her own game, Hilda seemed to stoop down to the child's behavior level and ordered a few of my coworkers to force the child to lie on her urine soaked mattress and bed sheets as punitive discipline. Needless to say, this went entirely against our policies as well as the driving purpose behind the existence of our center, which specifically was 'To Prevent Child Abuse and Neglect.' Regardless, Hilda did it anyway and instructed us all to "Keep this on the down low." Hilda then also further stated to us, apparently with full awareness and understanding of the inappropriate nature of her conduct, that "Management won't understand this."

At the time, I regret to admit that I reluctantly followed Hilda's orders and declined to report this terrible violation to management. Along with potentially facing more retaliation if I chose to report Hilda yet again, I was also concerned that my coworkers might not back me up in this instance. I felt this way because a few of the other child care providers had openly voiced their strong agreement with Hilda's repulsive method of treating this child, as they felt exasperated and believed the unusual discipline was warranted given this particular child's long-term, outrageous behavior.

Little did I realize it at the time, but Hilda's own long-term, outrageous behavior would soon be taking a turn for the worse.

Chapter Five

SMELL OF GENDER DISCRIMINATION

"You know how men are, they can never ask for help!" Bitterly spoken words by an angry Hilda Hullickson, expressed in my presence at the workplace, to a group of female employees.

Negative treatment from Hilda toward me continued into the year 2009. In early February of that year, I went on a three-month medical leave from work following surgery on my left shoulder.

When I eventually returned to work at the end of April 2009, I found that Hilda's personal life was the hottest topic of discussion among my coworkers. While I never wished to know intimate details about Hilda's ongoing drama with her male roommate outside of the workplace, it was impossible to avoid such exposure as Hilda complained about it frequently throughout each day at work. This remained a popular subject of discussion at work for nearly a month, from the end of April 2009 until the end of May 2009, when Hilda's male roommate reportedly booted her out of his apartment.

During this month-long time period, Hilda complained incessantly at work about how distraught she was at being thrown out of her male roommate's apartment; over her initially having no new place to go to; over his complaining about her being overweight; over his having another woman come over to the apartment; over his repeatedly calling the police on her for parking her car near his driveway; and about how very jilted the entire ordeal made her

28

feel. Furthermore, on some instances when talking openly in our employee office, Hilda made generalizing statements about the entire male gender in a negative manner… once in particular stating in a very bitter tone of voice that "YOU KNOW HOW MEN ARE, THEY CAN NEVER ASK FOR HELP!" This thundering, judgmental remark stood out in my mind and made me feel personally attacked and uncomfortable; being the only man in an office room full of females and ironically, also being a man who typically did not have a problem in asking for help.

Interestingly, beginning the very next month in June 2009, I suddenly found myself being unfairly accused; suspected; investigated; disciplined; and threatened with potential discipline on apparent allegations of child misconduct against me… all of which were first brought to my attention by none other than supervisor Hilda on the afternoon of Tuesday, June 16, 2009. These allegations against me also coincided with the arrival of a new Human Resources Director at our center, a woman who was quietly rumored as being a rather 'suspicious and possibly somewhat unprofessional' person through the employee grapevine. The Director's name was Claudia Cahill, and she had arrived at the center while I had been away on medical leave in February 2009.

As it turned out, the following two weeks were incredibly awful for me. On Monday, June 22, 2009, I sat down for a meeting with HR Director, Claudia Cahill; Children's Services Manager, Candy Rollins; and my union representative, Mack Sterling. During this most unusual hearing, Claudia went on to ask me a series of questions mostly having to do with information concerning my girlfriend and her son, Peter. Naturally, I was stunned and appalled at this line of questioning, along with questions over whether or not I had ever raised my voice while interacting with children at the center. My parents, who were on a trip to visit my brother in another state, felt compelled to cut their vacation short and return to support me through whatever was to come.

During the investigation that followed; a highly respected, long-term, senior coworker named Julie Worley, privately told me that she had been interviewed by the new HR Director, Claudia Cahill, and was personally asked by Claudia whether or not I was punitive toward the children at our center. Julie told me that she had told the truth, stood up for me, and had honestly told Claudia that "Sumi is not harsh or punitive toward children at the center." Julie further reassured me that she always tells the truth to management in work related matters, but that she would not want the HR Director Claudia to learn that she had confided to me about this interview. "I am afraid of retaliation from Claudia and I DO NOT want to be involved!" Julie had firmly stated. I assured Julie that I would keep it confidential, and honestly meant in good faith to do so.

However, for my own personal record, I still followed the professional advice of my mentor, Connie Cooper, and I documented exactly when and where this revealing conversation with Julie took place: It was Saturday, July 4, 2009, around 8:15 p.m. in the employee break room. I knew that sometime in the future, documentation of this conversation might become important to me in asserting my rights against this unfair employer. Should this matter ever rise to the level of going to court; I pondered, I might need to remember what Julie had said and exactly when, where, and how she had said it.

As it turned out; I was eventually disciplined on Monday, June 29, 2009, by Children's Services Manager, Candy Rollins; and NOT for any form of child misconduct mind you. Instead, I was reprimanded for having described the difficult life my girlfriend's young son Peter had experienced, and for having this conversation with curious volunteers who had asked why I had chosen this profession. As one of only three male child care providers employed at the center, and essentially the only one visible to most of our weekly volunteers, I was frequently asked this question by good natured people who were eager to know what had motivated an adult male to leave the hospitality industry to instead change diapers and care for small children.

Therefore, whenever asked this question; I felt honored to be able to talk about Peter in a triumphant manner and share how well he was now doing, due to my involvement in his life. I also did not speak in a loud or inappropriate manner in front of children as was apparently alleged, in which the children around us could have potentially become aware of some of the serious, adult nature of our conversations. I had simply answered the same old questions from our volunteers, and in the exact same manner, as I had now done throughout my two years of employment at the center. However, I alone was now specifically cited for discussing my 'personal life' with volunteers.

In short, I was utterly appalled at how cruelly and unfairly I had been treated. The thirteen days, June 16 – June 29, of not knowing my fate in this matter were stressful beyond what words can describe. To top it all off, there was absolutely no need whatsoever for any discipline or the lengthy 'investigation' into my conduct with children at the center. At the very most, perhaps an oral coaching or counseling from management would have been appropriate, but certainly not a disciplinary report that would remain in my personnel file for at least the next 12 months!

My union representative, Mack Sterling, enthusiastically agreed with my perceptions; and said that he felt the situation was "BS and unfair, but there's not a whole lot I can do." I also found it very disturbing that all of my female coworkers ALWAYS spoke freely in tremendous, similar detail about their families, children, and grandchildren; but were NEVER disciplined or threatened with potential discipline for doing so. In fact, some female colleagues laughed at me when I said I'd become afraid of discussing my personal life here at work!

Needless to say, I vented my mounting frustrations effectively by keeping up to date documentation of everything unfair that was happening. In fact, I soon began to document specific instances in which female staff members, including the supervisor, Hilda, herself; talked at great length with volunteers about personal matters without being punished for it. Someday, I figured, it might all become very useful as evidence of gender discrimination.

Along these lines things only proceeded to get worse as the summer of 2009 progressed. Hilda's harsh verbal reprimands toward me continued on a regular basis, with me documenting each specific incident for my own personal record. Hilda's age old attempts to strike at me through unfair discipline also continued during this time frame. On July 8, Hilda presented me with two new potential disciplinary items allegedly relating to my job performance. Since I requested union representation for the item which carried possible discipline, dealing with that one was postponed until a later day; again, I was not told what the allegation was about. On the non-disciplinary item, Hilda criticized me about how I wrote my daily logs describing the children's numerous activities. The criticism seemed quite unfounded, especially when I compared my daily logs with those of my female coworkers. Also, after getting permission from my union representative, Mack Sterling; on July 9, I asked several female colleagues if Hilda had taken issue recently with how they wrote their daily logs, and all replied to me by saying that Hilda had not taken issue with their daily logs.

Then on Wednesday, July 15, 2009, Hilda disciplined me during a union meeting over the second item; which was first brought to my attention exactly one week before. As it turned out, one of Hilda's close friends on the overnight staff, whom I will call Samantha Jackson; reported having found a small child with feces running down his groin, legs and feet. Samantha said this supposedly was found just moments after I had changed the child's diaper before leaving work. Although I honestly asserted that the child had been properly cleaned when I changed his diaper, it is of course a conceivable possibility that the child may have soiled himself again after my successful diaper change, Hilda failed to believe me and disciplined me on this item anyway with a written warning. Again, I felt helpless and intensely frustrated; but there wasn't much more that my union representative, Mack Sterling, was able to do.

Regardless of this setback, I continued to keep my behavior proactive. Later that same evening, on July 15; shortly after returning home from work early at 7 p.m., I spoke over the phone for about twenty minutes with a former receptionist who had recently left our center for a better job offer. I felt compelled to call her, as she had expressed her concerns to me over the ways in which I; along with another child care provider, whom I will call Jennifer Thompson, were being mistreated by the new HR Director. In fact, Jennifer had recently been terminated from her employment at the center; and many of us, including veteran employee Julie Worley and this former receptionist, had strong reason to believe that Jennifer's termination was completely unjust. When I noticed this ex-receptionist had left her phone number at her old work desk, I put on my detective hat and decided to see if she knew anything that might be of value to me.

And she certainly did! During our twenty-minute phone conversation, the ex-receptionist disclosed a whole lot of concerning information to me about Claudia Cahill; information that she claimed she had obtained by working very closely with Claudia as the center's receptionist over the past couple of months, from February 2009 through July 2009. This included information on how Claudia allegedly did not have the 'HR Specialist Degree' which Claudia claimed to have, and how Claudia had already once wrongfully fired and then had to rehire another long-term employee. The ex-receptionist also said she firmly believed that something shady had occurred regarding the manner in which Claudia left her previous job and obtained this one, and she specifically suggested that I ask the employee union to investigate this matter further.

She also said that Claudia had not kept up on my paperwork while I was off work for medical leave between the beginning of February 2009 to the end of April 2009, and that she had personally found many mistakes and errors on job applications and other work done by Claudia. The ex-receptionist also said that she personally believed that Claudia was unprofessional, and that there were a lot of shady and questionable things going on at the center.

Finally in closing, the ex-receptionist strongly advised me that I should continue to stand up for my rights and should not allow the center to take over my life and my soul. I thanked this recent ex-employee for her most revealing disclosures, and further empowered myself by documenting it all for my personal record. Knowledge is power, and this information provided me with an early indication that the new HR Director might not be up to any good.

Finally, on Sunday, July 19, 2009, Hilda yelled at me in the dining room over my not sitting right next to all three of the children whom I was assigned to look after. Even though I politely explained to Hilda that I had been bathing a different child upstairs on her previous orders, and that a volunteer had meanwhile already determined the children's seating arrangement; Hilda would not relent in her attack on my performance. "It doesn't matter where a volunteer or anyone else may have placed your child," Hilda said to me sternly. "Those three are YOUR three assigned children and YOU are responsible for sitting right next to all of them!"

Once Hilda had left the dining room, I decided to be proactive and approached two of my female coworkers and asked them separately if they were currently seated right next to all three of their assigned children. Both informed me that they were NOT indeed sitting right next to at least one of their assigned children. I then asked them if Hilda had said anything to them about this same exact issue, and they both told me that Hilda had NOT said a single word to them about this. I went on to document this incident in its entirety, including the names of the female staff people and the names of their assigned children whom they did not properly have seated beside them. Hilda also singled me out for verbal reprimands earlier on that same day, and again later toward the very end of my shift.

I, of course, had no desire to get any of my coworkers into trouble. However, having documented these latest of several similar incidents, I now felt as though I had enough evidence to formally accuse my supervisor of discriminatory behavior.

Chapter Six

THE GRIEVANCE THAT WASN'T AN ISSUE

"This is NOT my issue. These are NOT my issues." **Cut and dry statements from intimidating Children's Services Manager, Candy Rollins, in the center's official response to my July 2009 union grievance alleging gender discrimination.**

Mack Sterling was the representative from my employee union who had been handling my issues with supervisor Hilda during the summer of 2009. He was a highly talkative, easily excitable, young guy; probably in his late 20s to early 30s. But while Mack appeared to excel in the area of providing enthusiastic moral support for me, he seemed to lack when it came to having actual knowledge of some of the union's more complicated procedures. As a result, Mack recommended that I meet with his boss, a senior union representative named Lakisha Williams; to further discuss the option of filing a grievance against my supervisor.

So on Monday, July 20, 2009, my father and I met with Lakisha at a local restaurant for about an hour. As expected, Lakisha came across as an older, wiser and more knowledgeable representative of my employee union. She also appeared to be quite confident and sure of herself when it came to explaining what the union could potentially do to assist me.

Upon hearing details of my long-term harassment at the hands of supervisor Hilda, Lakisha firmly validated my perception and belief that I was being treated unfairly in a discriminatory manner. Over the course of the hour, Lakisha went on to explain to us that a grievance must be filed within eight days of the occurrence of a particular incident. Therefore, she suggested, we must file the grievance specifically over the dining room incident with Hilda; which occurred the previous day at work on Sunday, July 19. Though the grievance would be filed in relation to just this one incident, Lakisha said I would still be allowed to discuss Hilda's long-standing pattern of ongoing harassment and discriminatory behavior towards me.

With regards to the issue of discrimination in particular, Lakisha recommended to us that I also attempt to file a 'charge of discrimination' through the State Department of Human Rights (DHR). "That, in addition to filing the union grievance, would be the next step in the direction of taking legal action against your employer," Lakisha explained to us. And last, but certainly not the least, Lakisha solemnly warned us that "By filing a grievance alleging gender discrimination, you may actually observe an increase in harassment and reprisal towards you by both Hilda and the organization." While my father and I clearly saw the truth in this statement, we also realized that things were already quite bad and that I needed to take some form of action towards obtaining relief from Hilda's mistreatment. We ended the meeting with Lakisha telling us that "I will begin the process of filing your grievance. Mack Sterling will soon be in contact with you to further assist in this process."

This 'process,' as it turned out, would drag on for nearly two months. On Thursday, July 23, 2009; union representative, Mack Sterling officially filed my grievance with the center's HR Director, Claudia Cahill. One week later; on Thursday, July 30, 2009; Mack and I finally had our 'step one' grievance meeting with Children's Services Manager, Candy Rollins and another administrative staff member who sat in as a witness for Candy.

Along with discussing my personal issues relating to the grievance itself, there was another side issue that I felt compelled to bring up during this meeting. This had to do with an incident that occurred at the workplace on Friday, July 17, at about 4 p.m. It involved my observance of another staff member, whom I will call Crystal Matthews, verbally and physically mistreating a vulnerable child. This incident was particularly concerning to me, because staff member Crystal had a well noted history of abusive behaviors toward children at our center... yet, she was somehow still allowed to keep working there as a child care provider.

Immediately following the incident on Friday, July 17, I had submitted a written report about it directly to my supervisor Hilda Hullickson, as I was required to do by state law as a legally mandated reporter. Hilda, who herself was abusive to children; per my observations, appeared reluctant to process my report on my coworker Crystal's mistreatment of a child... as well as to deliver it to Children's Services Manager, Candy Rollins. Although Hilda promised me she would deliver the report on July 17, I had good reason to believe over the following weeks that Hilda had intentionally declined to do so. And at the beginning of the 'step one' grievance meeting on July 30, I was able to confirm my hunch upon confronting Children's Services Manager, Candy Rollins about this issue. It came as no surprise to me when Candy appeared stunned and said she had no knowledge of the incident I was now describing, which had occurred nearly a full two weeks earlier on Friday, July 17!

Having addressed this first unrelated issue, I then proceeded to share my lengthy documentation of events regarding Hilda's mistreatment of me with Children's Services Manager, Candy Rollins. More than anything else, Candy appeared overwhelmed and blown away at the amount of detail I was able to present outlining the dates and times of numerous incidents perpetrated toward me by Hilda. Candy sighed heavily several times and practically pleaded with my union representative to be given more time to process all of my information.

Next came a second 'step two' grievance meeting on Thursday, August 20, 2009. Again, participants at this meeting included Children's Services Manager, Candy Rollins; union representative, Mack Sterling; and I. Unlike her honestly baffled reaction at the July 30th meeting, Candy aggressively defended Hilda's misconduct this time by asserting that this was not her problem to deal with. "This is NOT my issue. These are NOT my issues!" were the defiant words which Candy dryly spoke as being the center's official response to my union grievance alleging gender discrimination. Mack Sterling and I both glanced at each other in disbelief as Candy continued on with her hollow remarks by further stating, "If I was the person whom Sumi was accusing of all this stuff, then this would be my issue. However, I am usually at home and not even in the building when Sumi claims all of this negative stuff with his supervisor, Hilda, is allegedly occurring. So therefore, this is simply NOT my issue."

As an answer in written form to my union grievance, an irritated Candy handed us a short memo which meagerly stated, "An investigation of your concerns was conducted. I appreciate the opportunity to look into your concerns." Needless to say, this response was viewed as highly inadequate by Mack Sterling, Lakisha Williams and me; especially considering the fact that incidents of Hilda's discriminatory behavior toward me had in turn continued. Though frustrated and exasperated, I continued to work with Mack Sterling and to document everything that happened on this particularly awful day at work; especially noting Candy's brazen, nonsensical declaration as the Children's Services Manager that this simply wasn't 'her issue' to deal with.

At long last, there was finally a 'step three' grievance meeting on Tuesday, September 1, 2009. This time senior union representative, Lakisha Williams herself was present at the meeting, along with junior union representative, Mack Sterling and I. Candy Rollins was absent this time and replaced by HR Director, Claudia Cahill. In stark contrast to Candy's dismissive approach on August 20, Claudia surprisingly acknowledged Hilda's poor treatment of me. Claudia even went on to characterize Hilda's behavior as being an "unintentional lack of impulse control," but she conveniently stopped short of agreeing that it amounted to gender discrimination. Throughout the meeting, Claudia appeared to be intimidated by the confident manner in which Lakisha spoke about the situation. In fact, at one point; Lakisha got Claudia to reluctantly admit that, as an organization, "We do indeed have a lot of work to do with training Hilda better."

Unfortunately, Claudia's actions would soon speak a whole lot louder than her positive words at this meeting. The incidents with Hilda proceeded to continue, as I had correctly predicted they would. However, there were two new occurrences which did surprise me considerably. First off, HR Director, Claudia inexplicably turned on me like a venomous snake; and much like Candy, she began to blame me entirely for my ongoing problems with Hilda. Also just as devastating; was the fact that senior union representative, Lakisha Williams; suddenly declined to support me with the same interest, energy and enthusiasm as she had displayed before. Although she had preached to me strongly to not allow myself to 'become a victim,' Lakisha suddenly appeared unwilling to respond when I asked her to do her job as my union representative and help me with asserting my rights in an appropriate manner.

Soon there would be a new incident where Hilda yelled at me, and then with Claudia's backing, Hilda proceeded to discipline me for following Mack's advice and politely standing up for myself! Eventually, I had to file another union grievance with Mack's help to get this particular 'written warning' successfully reduced to a less serious status of just being an 'oral coaching.' I also found myself being wrongly accused, once again, of having a supposedly 'inappropriate' conversation with a volunteer on the center's playground. On Monday, September 21, I was ordered by Hilda to no longer discuss my personal life at the workplace. Mack said he felt this unusual directive was discriminatory in nature, as it appeared to only apply to me. He strongly suggested that I continue to document such behavior by Hilda and the center's management.

In spite of these hassles, there was hope that all my documentation might eventually pay off. Along with filing the grievance on July 23, I had successfully filled out an Employment Discrimination Questionnaire (EDQ), and mailed it into the DHR in early August 2009. Along with answering the department's list of standard questions, I was able to submit ALL of my highly detailed, meticulous documentation to the department along with the questionnaire itself. I had also spoken with an attorney around this point in time, and the lawyer was encouraging about grounds for a case against my employer… especially when and if the DHR was able to draft for me a charge of discrimination.

Regardless of the outcome of these various steps, one thing had become painfully clear to me; as senior union representative, Lakisha Williams herself would relay to me over the following months during a phone conversation, "No amount or number of grievances are going to resolve these issues."

Chapter Seven

HILDA'S MISCONDUCT WITH CHILDREN CONTINUES

"Remember, you are still a mandated reporter and are still required to keep doing your job in this regard!" **Statement made to me in December 2009 by lead investigator at the Department of Human Services (DHS), the state agency that licenses the center to operate.**

As the fall of 2009 progressed, I noticed that supervisor Hilda Hullickson's mistreatment of the children at our center began to resurface. On Friday, October 9, 2009; Hilda allowed a recently fired, ex-employee to enter our secure building after management had gone home for the weekend. The ex-employee was apparently a personal friend of Hilda's, and was no longer authorized to be inside our locked building following her termination. The reality of this common-sense boundary appeared to be lost on Hilda.

On the contrary, our supervisor then did something that seemed to me to be a much more serious violation of company policy. She instructed the unauthorized visitor to perform one on one child care duties on our shift. According to the basic rules at our center; the children must ALWAYS be observed by proper, qualified individuals at ALL times; and not by someone who was not a member of the staff at that time. At one point during the evening,

42

I even observed that the unauthorized visitor had been left alone in a small room in charge of four youngsters for several minutes!

Concerned about the ramifications such a licensing violation could potentially have on the future operation of our center, I telephoned Children's Services Manager, Candy Rollins during my 15-minute break that evening and told her what was occurring. Within minutes, a concerned looking HR Director, Claudia Cahill had entered the building; and according to one of my coworkers, had sternly escorted the former employee out of our secure center.

However, Claudia was much less critical of supervisor Hilda's extremely poor judgment in creating this entire situation. In contrast to her reported abrasiveness toward the unauthorized visitor, Claudia seemed unusually meek and sympathetic when I observed her confronting Hilda about this. Hilda, in response to seeing Claudia, simply shrugged the incident off and replied by saying "Yeah, yeah. That was my fault. That was me." All stated with the nonchalant self-assurance that she would not be reprimanded for this huge breach of building security, a very serious policy violation; which would have likely resulted in the immediate suspension and termination of anyone else besides, apparently, our PM shift supervisor. Hilda clearly seemed to be above the rule of law.

As had become standard procedure for me by this point in time; I documented the above-mentioned incident in full detail that same Friday evening after my shift, including names of all other witnesses besides me. Only this time instead of sending the write-up to Candy or Claudia, who were both already aware of what had occurred; I decided to email it directly to our center's Executive Director, Karen Patrick. By doing so, it was my profound hope that the top individual in management would perhaps be more likely to address this particular incident with the level of seriousness that it deserved.

At first it seemed as though this might actually occur. On Monday, October 12, 2009, Karen Patrick approached me at the workplace and quietly whispered the words, "Thank You" to me, accompanied with a knowing nod and a smile. However, in the days and weeks that followed, our Executive Director never provided me with any assurance that measures were being taken by management to prevent a potential reoccurrence of events. I felt a reoccurrence of the scenario was indeed quite probable, as Hilda was the PM shift supervisor and regularly worked on evenings and weekends when management was simply not around. I remained bothered by the notion that an unauthorized individual, essentially any random person off the streets, could again be allowed to walk into our secured building and be left alone to care for the children entrusted to us.

Acting on the advice of my mentor, Connie Cooper, I decided that I should consider bringing my concerns to the attention of our center's Board of Directors; a bold and gutsy move which would involve going over the heads of our Executive Director and the managers within the building. While I naturally felt reluctant to do this, I also felt genuinely concerned that management was intentionally covering up Hilda's misconduct and would simply continue to do so. And since the slogan commonly used for our center was that "THE CHILDREN MUST ALWAYS COME FIRST," I concluded that it was now time for me to live up to that high expectation.

Very, very fortunately, I did some important studying before actually taking any action. In fact, if I am to be more truthful, it was really all my girlfriend's idea to do a little research first. On her own initiative, my girlfriend opened my employee handbook and started to read up on all of the company's many rules and regulations. Like most average folks, I had never read through the entire handbook, as I never dreamed I would need to be keenly aware of all the tiny fine print. However, by doing so now, I was able to empower myself in a way I could have never previously imagined.

Following my girlfriend's lead, I read up on the section in the handbook which described "Good Faith Reporting." In regards to reporting a concern to our management, the book instructed that "Employees should document any incident they find harmful and submit the documentation to their supervisor or appropriate person. In the event the supervisor does not make a response, the complaint should then be directed to the Executive Director. If there is still no response, the Chair of the Board of Directors should be notified."

Obviously, I was not going to inform the supervisor in this instance, since she was the one causing the specific problem at hand. And although the Executive Director had thanked me personally for my detailed email to her, she had not provided me with any response as to what management was doing to ensure the future safety of the children. Therefore, I decided to follow my mentor's advice and contacted the Chair of the Board of Directors. While I feared retaliation from management for doing so, I happened to read the next paragraph in the handbook. This introduced me to the Whistleblower Protection Act of 1989, which covers all employees. It went on to specifically state that *Employees who act in good faith cannot be the target of retaliation for reporting or documenting acts they believe to be harmful. Further, EEOC (Equal Employment Opportunity Commission) confirms that it is a violation of the law for anyone to retaliate against an employee because they are opposed to what the employee has reasonably and in good faith reported to be unlawful discrimination or sexual harassment. Retaliation shall not occur because an employee has made a charge, filed a complaint, testified or participated in an investigation, proceeding or hearing.*

Reading this immediately made me feel more secure about my decision to have formally accused my supervisor of gender discrimination with the grievance I had filed in July.

Along with suggesting that I approach the Board of Directors, my mentor Connie Cooper had also advised me to report this latest incident created by Hilda to the DHS. Though I was again initially concerned about facing retaliation from management for doing this, I felt enlightened when I read the following statement in the next paragraph of my employee handbook, which specifically stated: "Concerns and complaints made to the DHS shall be respected and no retaliation shall occur. This organization encourages employees to report all incidents to the DHS that puts any child at risk or is harmful to their physical or emotional safety."

Based on having empowered myself with this specific legal knowledge, I went ahead and reported the October 9 incident to both the Chair of the Board of Directors as well as to the DHS. If I were to be fired as a result of this reporting, I was now aware that I would likely have some strong legal claims against my employer. To further ensure that action would be taken, I also sent a copy of the report to the Vice Chair of the Board as well. While the DHS responded by saying their investigation into the incident would likely take a very long time to complete, the Chair and Vice Chair both responded to me and said that I'd receive a follow up letter.

Eventually in early December 2009, I received a follow-up letter from the organization's attorney regarding this matter. The message started out with a reassuring statement by the lawyer on the company's behalf, which stated "Let me assure you that your fears of retaliation are unfounded." While clearly admitting that Hilda's actions in this incident were indeed 'wrong and inappropriate,' the letter also attempted to downplay the significance of this serious company violation. It eventually proceeded to conclude that "The supervisor on duty that night

46

has been warned to adhere to the building's policy concerning visitors, and we feel confident that the scenario will not occur again in the future. At this time, the organization cannot think of any other action it can take in response to this incident."

Right around this same point in time, I got a call from the DHS investigators and went in for a two-hour interview with them on Wednesday, December 2, 2009. During this interview, I went on to inform the DHS about my observations of all of supervisor Hilda's previous misconduct with children over the years within our organization. The investigators seemed very serious about wishing to look into this; as well as investigating my coworker, Crystal Matthews. Crystal also seemed to have a long history of mistreating children and was responsible, per my observations; for the July 17, 2009, mistreatment of a child in our care. This was the earlier incident I refer to where I had written a report and Hilda apparently concealed it from the Children's Services Manager. I also provided the DHS with the names and contact info of several other eyewitnesses, including my good friend and ally, Mary Monahan who had observed the mistreatment of children by both Hilda and Crystal Matthews. However, as they told me before, the DHS warned that their investigation would take a very long period of time to complete. In the meantime, they instructed me to continue to report any new incidents which occurred. "Remember, you are *still* a mandated reporter and are still required to keep doing your job in this regard!" the lead DHS investigator firmly stated to me.

And new incidents with the increasingly brazen Hilda would continue to unfold. Over the weekend of Friday, December 18, 2009, I observed that Hilda targeted a four-year-old girl and her two year old brother with major verbal and physical aggression. What was most disturbing about these particular incidents, was the fact that Hilda did this after I had informed her that the four-year-old girl just claimed to have suffered recent abuse from her mother! When I first told Hilda about this, she appeared angry and frustrated that I was following proper protocol and that we needed to call Child Protective Services (CPS) to report the alleged abuse.

After reluctantly agreeing that we must indeed call CPS, I noticed that Hilda grew extremely agitated toward this particular child and her little brother and remained so on Friday as well as two days later on Sunday, December 20, 2009. Hilda's hostile conduct over these two days, per my observations; included slamming a chair down hard right in front of the terrified girl, pulling hard on the girl and her little brother's arms, hollering at the girl and her little brother unnecessarily; as far as I could see, and then taking both children into a small linen closet with a lock on the door where staff are NEVER allowed to take children. What was equally disturbing to me, was how I noticed the other staff and volunteers simply choosing to look the other way as much of this was occurring.

I, however, once again refused to look the other way in spite of the risk to my job. After my shift that Sunday evening, I sent a lengthy, detailed email to the Children's Services Manager, the HR Director, the Executive Director and also again to the Chair of the Board of Directors. I also proceeded to mail my written report to the DHS.

While I knew in my heart that I was doing the right thing, I had never really experienced all out retaliation before. Soon I would discover the price one must pay when deciding to be a whistleblower.

Chapter Eight

THE HIGH PRICE OF WHISTLEBLOWING PART ONE: FEELING MY MANAGERS' WRATH

"I don't give people hell. I just tell them the truth and they think it is hell." **Profound statement made by Harry Truman, which I found applies exactly to the role of a whistleblower in the workplace.**

Even before I brought concerns about Hilda to the Chair of the Board of Directors for the second time, I had already begun to experience what seemed to be retaliation for my whistle-blowing activities. This occurred in early- to mid-December 2009; and in this instance, it appeared as though Hilda's close buddy, Samantha Jackson, a regular on the overnight shift who had reported me over an alleged diapering infraction in July; had been the individual behind it once again. Although I had grown somewhat accustomed to unfair treatment by this point, even I could not have foreseen exactly how bad things were soon going to get.

During the second half of the evening shift on Monday, December 14, Hilda's pal Samantha had come in early to fill in for someone else, before beginning her regular overnight shift at 10:45 p.m. At about 7:45 p.m., we brought the children into an activity room and sat them down to watch a movie... a regular routine at the center before we brought the children upstairs for bedtime. There were several other adults downstairs in the activity room with me, and as usual there was an overflow of children. Since all of the children could not fit on the sitting space available on the carpet, some of the staff and volunteers would often allow the remaining children to sit on their laps for the duration of the movie. As we seated the children; it appeared that there were two very little girls, sisters who were about two-years-old and eighteen-months respectively, who could not find any space to sit on the carpet. Since all of the other adults in the room, including Samantha, already had at least one child physically sitting on them, I readily allowed these last two children to come over and sit on my lap.

To my great surprise, Samantha immediately voiced her strong personal objections to this. "You can't have them on your lap... GET THEM OFF YOUR LAP!" Samantha demanded of me. I was taken aback at this authoritative comment rudely made by Samantha, as she was not one of my superiors but was rather a same level employee. I politely informed Samantha that I, along with all other child care providers and all volunteers, have always been permitted and encouraged by the center to allow children to cuddle and sit on our laps. This had been the case since my days as child care "Volunteer of the Year" and throughout my employment as a child care provider. I also politely asked Samantha why she was directing her statement specifically toward ONLY ME, when there were several other female staff members and female volunteers who also had children currently sitting on their laps, including Samantha herself. Samantha did not have a clear answer for me, but responded by saying, "I just personally do not think that it is a smart idea for you, Sumi, to have children sit on your lap. This isn't my normal shift and I don't know how you guys do things on the evening shift, but that is simply my personal opinion." Now had there been a company rule in place prohibiting males from having children sit in their laps, I certainly would have adhered to it. But there was no such rule or policy at our center. Clearly, I felt as though Hilda's pal had singled me out in this instance because of my gender as a male.

While Samantha did proceed to back off after I politely asserted myself, this would not be the last time I heard about this issue. Two days later on Wednesday, December 16, I was instructed to report to the office of the center's HR Director, Claudia Cahill. Although I had been previously told that Claudia was going to follow up with me on some recent concerns I had voiced about Hilda, Claudia clearly had a much different agenda in mind for me.

Upon entering her office, Claudia firmly informed me that she had received two written complaints about my job performance from another employee, in the form of two pink write-up sheets. The first item had to do with my allegedly having failed to change a child's diaper in a timely fashion. The second item, to my utter shock and dismay, was a report that I had allegedly allowed little children to "jump and crawl on my lap" in a manner that was reportedly viewed by the 'individual' who disclosed it as being "inappropriate." Obviously, it was clear to me that the allegations made in this report had been generated by Samantha and had never occurred, and when I reacted with great concern and asserted that no inappropriate activity had taken place, Claudia clearly appeared to not believe me. "You refused to communicate appropriately with your coworkers, Sumi! You mustn't allow children to jump on your lap!" Claudia strongly stated to me. Perceiving that I was being unfairly disciplined at this point on a serious, false accusation with disturbing implications, I repeatedly requested Claudia to allow me to have my union representative, Mack Sterling, present for this meeting. As employees at the center, we were entitled to have a union representative present when and if we were receiving any form of discipline. I also told Claudia that I felt as though I was experiencing retaliation now for recent complaints I had made about Hilda.

51

At this point, the previously accusing Claudia suddenly changed her tune and responded to me by saying, "Oh Sumi, look at how you are acting? This is not a disciplinary meeting! I am merely trying to communicate with you, but you are refusing to communicate with me." Then using a tone of voice that an adult would typically use to convey insincere pity towards an unhappy child, Claudia continued by saying to me "Oh Sumi... it must be so hard for you to not be able to communicate normally with your coworkers. I am concerned about your attitude and your ability to perform your job duties."

Needless to say, I was tremendously shaken up following this horrible encounter with Claudia. Clearly, this did NOT appear to be the proper, professional manner in which a Human Resources Director was supposed to act or investigate potential allegations. I felt that if Claudia had the wisdom or common sense to interview the other adults who were present in the activity room on Monday evening, she would have quickly learned firsthand that absolutely nothing inappropriate had occurred. But instead, just as the ex-receptionist had conveyed to me in July, Claudia did not appear to be aware of how to conduct her duties as an HR Director.

In response to this meeting, I immediately talked to my dad and we made an appointment to see a lawyer. This was the employment law attorney whom my dad had spoken with briefly over the phone after I filed the grievance against Hilda in July. On Friday, December 18, my dad and I had a meeting with this lawyer. In this meeting, I came to understand that due to my extensive and up-to-date documentation, I had grounds to make a case against my employer for discriminatory harassment. However, based on our discussions at this meeting, we decided to continue to wait for the DHR to return a charge of discrimination in response to the EDQ I had submitted in August. I also understood from this meeting that it was important for me to keep on doing my job correctly, remaining polite and cooperative with management and to continue my documentation while maintaining contact with my lawyer as needed.

Shortly after our meeting on that same Friday morning, I had a phone conversation with my union representative, Mack Sterling. During this conversation, Mack made a personal prediction to me that he believed the center's management would soon attempt to unfairly discipline me over a diapering related incident, specifically to try to get three of the same write- ups against me and then justify having me fired. I also told Mack what had recently happened about Samantha making the accusation about children "jumping and crawling on my lap in an inappropriate manner," and about how Claudia had reacted to it. Mack then stated his personal belief that Hilda was turning female coworkers against me so that Hilda "can sit back and say that reports about Sumi are coming to management from other employees and technically not coming from her." This made sense to me, as I had witnessed Hilda and Samantha having private conversations in Hilda's office on recent evenings before leaving work. At any rate, Mack remained very supportive of me and my position in these ongoing matters. This was not the case four days later on Tuesday, December 22, 2009; when I was summoned to the manager's office for a meeting regarding my second complaint to the center's Chair of the Board of Directors, this one concerning Hilda's atrocious behavior over the weekend. At this meeting, Claudia lost her temper and exploded towards me with wrath; all the while, Children's Services Manager, Candy Rollins observed our interaction with a surprised, half smirk on her face. "Now Sumi, YOU ARE NOT TO EVER, EVER REPORT ANYTHING TO THE BOARD OF DIRECTORS AGAIN, UNDERSTOOD?!" Claudia shouted as she pointed a long, accusing finger at me. "I am very concerned about the future of your employment here, Sumi!" Claudia proceeded to say in an overdramatic tone.

Incredibly, Claudia then blamed me for not having attempted to open the door to the linen closet where Hilda had led the two small children on Sunday, instead of properly placing focus on WHY Hilda had bullied the young siblings all weekend and WHY she had brought them into a room with a lock on the door. It seemed as though Claudia preferred to just shoot the messenger rather than appropriately addressing the much larger issues, concerning Hilda's inappropriate behaviors, which were staring her in the face. Along with further chiding me for my alleged failure to communicate properly, Claudia then ridiculed me for requesting to have a union representative present during the one-sided meeting on December 16. "You're a grown man, Sumi, and Mack cannot always be here to hold your hand," Claudia said to me in a taunting tone of voice.

But the worst part of this hideous meeting, by far; was the fact that my union representative, Mack Sterling, just sat there looking scared and refused to defend me at all. On the contrary, as I attempted to explain myself, Mack now began to agree with everything that Claudia was saying; and proceeded to roll his eyes and scoff when I was making my points. Seeing that I was suddenly outnumbered three to one, I recalled words of wisdom from my attorney, and I kept my cool under pressure. As it turned out, Claudia went on to inform me that I was not actually receiving any disciplinary actions during this meeting, in spite of the verbal tongue lashing. "If you ever go to the board of directors again Sumi then disciplinary action will follow," Claudia sternly warned me. "You must follow the proper chain of command from here on, and can only bring concerns about Hilda to her immediate supervisor, Candy Rollins." Interestingly, both Claudia and Candy appeared surprised when I remained calm and politely replied that I would indeed follow the proper chain of command in the future. It appeared as though the managers hoped that I would either fight back or just quit.

Although I did not argue or quit, I was utterly devastated by the way I had been treated. I couldn't understand how and why Mack's attitude had changed so drastically over four days. I wondered if Claudia had threatened Mack in some way, shape or form; perhaps with some punitive action against him as a union member. I just couldn't get past Mack's negative behavior, while he had been the one who was encouraging me to take legal action and 'sue the center!' But fearing that I might lose my cool and blow up, I decided not to confront Mack about this after the meeting. Given the circumstances it seemed pointless to do so. Especially in the aftermath of this meeting, I feared that whatever I said could be twisted by management and quickly used against me. Suddenly, I no longer knew who I could trust. Besides, I was feeling quite discouraged and beaten at that moment. Without a doubt, this was one of the very worst days I'd encountered thus far in my awful ordeal. I even broke down later that same afternoon, feeling as though a bully had defeated me yet again.

One small victory that I could soon claim in all this, however, was the fact that Hilda was taken out of the supervisor position shortly after my latest report to the Chair of the Board in December 2009. Regardless, the center's management still attempted to sugarcoat the truth about this matter, and instead proudly announced in the employee newsletter that Hilda would soon be pursuing a 'new opportunity' here at the workplace; this consisting of her stepping down in rank from the supervisor role to being a regular shift leader. Still, I saw Hilda's 'new opportunity' as a step in the right direction. A small step, however, as Hilda would continue to interact with the children just as much as when she'd been the supervisor, if not even more. I felt that the children, in essence, would continue to remain at risk.

And apparently so would I. As the new year of 2010 began, I continued to experience hostility directed toward me by Hilda. So in accordance with following the proper chain of command, I submitted a long letter to Children's Services Manager, Candy Rollins on Wednesday, January 6, 2010.

As it turned out, I did hear back from the center's management regarding this matter. During my shift on Thursday, January 7, Candy and Claudia called me into the office for what would gratefully be a very brief meeting. On this occasion, Claudia remained a silent observer while Candy merely acknowledged receiving my letter and instructed me to continue to do my job in a positive manner. It was yet another interesting answer from management in response to this long-term, ongoing issue of discriminatory harassment toward me from Hilda. Apparently, Candy still did not believe that this was 'her issue.'

However, management's more genuine response to this complaint came one day later; on Friday, January 8, 2010; and it presented itself in the form of retaliation. Upon arriving at the workplace, I was summoned to the office for a disciplinary meeting with Candy; Hilda; and my fabulously helpful union representative, Mack Sterling. Conducting the meeting, Hilda proceeded to give me two new written warnings; one for allegedly not changing a child's diaper in a timely fashion and the other for raising my voice in an allegedly 'threatening and shaming' manner toward a child.

Although Mack did little to defend me during this meeting, his behavior outside the building was even more confusing. As I phoned my dad to update him on what had occurred, Mack approached me and attempted to meagerly apologize for not having supported me during the meeting on December 22. When I turned away and refused to speak to him, Mack made the following statement to me anyway: "I just want to warn you and let you know, Sumi, THEY ARE COMING AFTER YOU!"

As always; I made sure to document this revealing disclosure from Mack, in regard to Hilda and the center's management, along with the discipline I had received. As it turned out, I was bullied further by Hilda yet again on that very same evening, and I strongly but politely responded by telling her to treat me with respect.

Although it felt good to stand up for myself, I knew that my future at the center looked bleak. Hilda and her bosses were gunning for me, and it would only be a matter of time before one of their bullets would hit.

Chapter Nine

THE HIGH PRICE OF WHISTLEBLOWING PART TWO: THE MAN CAN NO LONGER GIVE BATHS

"Now you haven't done something wrong that would prevent you from bathing children, have you Sumi? Because if you had done something, you would already be gone from here, right?"
Revealing statements made to me by a confused coworker at the center, showing that there had been a false belief spread among staff that there was a 'good reason' why I was not being assigned to bathe children.

By January 2010, I had spent the past several months meticulously keeping track of the manner in which I was being mistreated at work. In spite of my overall vigilance in this regard, there was one change in particular that I did not come to spot right away.

Shortly after Samantha's report to management about children sitting on my lap in mid-December, I began to notice that I was no longer being assigned to bathe children at the center. As paid child care providers with this company, we were all required to give baths to children on an almost daily basis. On busy afternoons and evenings, we could easily find ourselves each assigned to give multiple baths over the course of an eight hour shift. This is how it had been for me over the past two and a half years of my employment. However for a whole month, from the end of December 2009 until the end of January 2010; I found I was not assigned to bathe children on any shift that Hilda, specifically, was leading.

Soon there would be times when the children whom I was assigned to care for simply went without baths as the evening progressed. When I would call Hilda in her office and remind her that these children still needed their baths, Hilda would strangely respond to me by saying, "Oh don't worry about it, Sumi. We will take care of it." This made me feel great concern, as I suspected that the managers were trying to generate an implication among staff that there was a reason why I was not giving baths anymore. Following the 'lap sitting' issue that Samantha created in December; I began to wonder whether management was intentionally trying to portray me, the only male on my shift, in a negative light. Along these lines, I feared that perhaps they were trying to build a case for termination of my employment, based on spreading the false idea that I was somehow unsafe around kids.

Shockingly, I would soon come to learn that my concerns were right on the mark! This occurred on Friday, January 22, as I and another staff member entered into a conversation while supervising children in an activity room. The other staff member, whom I will call Susie Parker, found herself assigned to give baths to children who should have been assigned to my care. Appearing annoyed and confused, Susie repeatedly asked me why I had not been assigned to bathe kids anymore.

I replied by telling Susie that I did not know *why* I had not been assigned to bathe children. Susie did not appear satisfied with my answer, and urged me to call up to the shift leader and ask for more clarification. The shift leader on this evening, a lady whom I will call Toni Wilson, merely replied that Hilda was the one who had made the bathing assignments and that we needed to follow her orders. When I relayed this information to Susie, she gave me a strange look and then made the following statements to me which I will never forget: "Now you haven't done something wrong that would prevent you from bathing children, have you Sumi? Because if you had done something, you would already be gone from here, right?"

I was astonished at Susie's remarks and the strange, unnerving look that she shot at me; essentially questioning whether or not I may have molested or harmed a small child! When I immediately asked Susie where she got such a negative notion about me, the truth was finally revealed. "There was a night about a month ago when I was having a stressful evening and was burdened with having to bathe your children on top of my own," Susie told me. "So feeling frustrated, I asked Hilda if there was a reason why Sumi cannot give baths to his own assigned kids," Susie continued. "At that point, Hilda responded by telling me strongly that 'SUMI KNOWS EXACTLY WHY HE IS NOT ALLOWED TO GIVE CHILDREN BATHS ANYMORE!'"

Needless to say I was extremely distraught after hearing this shocking disclosure from Susie, which legally amounts to slander and defamation of character against me. When I then told Susie that I was about to confront Hilda, Susie repeatedly pleaded with me to not mention her name as being the one who provided this information. "Whatever's going on Sumi, I DO NOT want to be involved. I am afraid of getting in trouble with Hilda and facing retaliation for speaking out, so PLEASE DO NOT MENTION MY NAME when you talk to her!" While I said I would attempt to honor Susie's request, I made a mental note to document Susie's remarks right away after work, along with documenting the names of another staff member and a volunteer who were present in the room and had also witnessed Susie make her disclosure to me. I kept in mind that if this case someday went into court, Susie and these other eyewitnesses could be required to testify under oath about this revealing conversation.

But for the time being, I had more investigating to do. After excusing myself from the room, I immediately went upstairs and attempted to locate Hilda. Though Hilda had already left the building, shift leader Toni Wilson further validated Susie's statements by saying that she, too, was aware of a directive from Hilda to not allow me to give children baths. When I asked Toni more questions about this, she simply responded by saying, "All I know is what Hilda has told me. Hilda is the person who you need to speak with about this." Again, I made a mental note to document Toni's revealing statements right after work.

And just when one might think this particular evening could not get any worse, I had yet another negative encounter with Hilda's pal, Samantha Jackson. Upon entering the child care office and punching in to begin her overnight shift, Samantha started a conversation with some of the other female staff members. With me being the only male in an office room full of females, Samantha proceeded to make the following judgmental remarks about the male gender: "Men take such a long time to grow up. They don't grow up until they are at least forty-years-old!" Though I was already offended, given Samantha's history of singling me out based on gender and trying to get me into trouble; Samantha then proceeded to put me on the spot and directly asked me, "Well Sumi, you're a man, so how old are you?" When I politely replied that I was thirty-three, Samantha responded to this by loudly declaring, "Well, I know some men who don't grow up until they are fifty-seven years old!"

At this point, several of the female staff members laughed and began to jump into the conversation with negative comments and/or stories about men and our alleged lack of maturity as a gender. Most of them likely did not mean it, I figured, but it left me with a bad feeling. Though intensely frustrated on the inside, I remained calm and did not confront Samantha or create a scene in the office. It was simply not practical for one thing, as I found myself completely outnumbered by women! But on a more serious note; I felt that my decision to turn the other cheek was the best means by which I could prove to myself, if not to all of them, that I certainly did not fit their shallow depiction of men. Not to gloat now, but Bravo to me. I proved that I wasn't the immature one in that room.

What I did do, however, was send a politely worded letter about this incident to Children's Services Manager, Candy Rollins, on Monday, January 25, 2010. In this letter, I also shared my concerns about what I had heard from my female coworkers regarding Hilda's alleged directive prohibiting me, her only male employee, from being allowed to bathe children as my job duty requires. Due to what I had learned from filing the grievance in July; I now knew that it is illegal for an employer to terminate or punish an employee who comes forward to report what they perceive to be either sexual harassment or discrimination occurring at the workplace, so long as they report it in good faith, just as I was now doing. Hilda's alleged directive, prohibiting me only from giving children baths, displayed markedly different treatment toward me as opposed to how my female colleagues were treated. And the negative comments that Samantha made about men in my presence, and to me specifically; were also discriminatory in nature and specifically directed toward my gender, which is a protected class status. The comments had made me feel offended, put down, embarrassed and insulted. I knew reporting this now could give me grounds for a case if they fired me anytime soon.

The following material presented here is from the DHR website in 2010:

What is Illegal Discrimination? How are Your Rights Protected?

Not every act that is unfair or unreasonable is illegal. To be considered unlawful under the Human Rights Act (HRA), the discrimination must have happened because of one of the following reasons: race, color, creed, religion, national origin, sex, sexual orientation, marital status, physical or mental disability, receipt of public assistance, age, family status (housing only), and Human Rights Commission activity (employment only). These personal characteristics are also called "protected classes."

Does that mean that only some people — and not others — are protected by the Human Rights Act? No: the Human Rights Act protects everyone, because everyone has a race, sex, and many of the other characteristics that are covered.

The Act prohibits reprisal of retaliation because a person opposed a practice forbidden by the HRA, filed a charge or participated in a matter brought under the Act; or because a person associated with a person or group of persons who are disabled or of a different race, color, creed, religion, sexual orientation, or national origin.

The info I have listed above, obtained directly from the DHR website, explains what qualifies as being a 'Protected Class Status' under the HRA. The section concerning reprisal, explains how it is illegal to retaliate against an individual for opposing what they honestly believe to be a form of discrimination, in relation to a violation of a Protected Class Status. This is why I addressed my letter of January 25 to the center's management as "Disclosing what I believe, in good faith, to be unlawful gender discrimination against me at the workplace." If I were to be fired anytime soon after submitting this letter to Children's Services Manager, Candy Rollins, I knew I could present a strong argument that my termination was based on retaliation and therefore was illegal and in violation of the HRA.

On Tuesday, January 26, 2010; the HR Director, Claudia Cahill, approached me over the letter I had submitted to Candy. Apparently playing the role of 'good cop' for the moment, Claudia assured me that Samantha's actions were indeed "inappropriate conduct which cannot occur or be tolerated at the workplace." Attempting to display concern and emotion, Claudia dramatically vowed that she would speak with Samantha immediately regarding this issue. Interestingly there was no comment from Claudia, however, in regard to my concerns about Hilda's alleged directive to prohibit me from giving baths to children at the center.

I was then subsequently called into a meeting room with none other than Candy and Hilda, herself. Although I was not receiving any disciplinary action, Hilda had wished to inform me that she had allegedly found a child who had been in my care the previous night to be "unclean, with dirt on her hair, back and neck," after I had left work at 11:00 p.m. Though I confirmed again that I was not being disciplined, Hilda claimed she had wanted to bring this to my attention.

Seeing that the two of them were in a discussion mood, I then asked Candy if I could open our conversation up to the subject concerning what another staff person had recently told me in regard to the child bathing issue. Before I could elaborate any further, I immediately observed that Hilda suddenly began to look red-faced and nervous. It was clear to me that she was frightened, it was such a rare occurrence to witness fear on the face of the person who most often instilled fear in others!

Without referring to my coworker Susie by name, I informed both women that a trusted colleague had reported to me that Hilda had placed a ban on my ability to give baths to children, and that Hilda had further implied that there was a good reason for such a ban to be in place against me. Although now appearing very nervous, Hilda proceeded to deny that any such ban was ever in place, and she asserted that there was no reason that I would not be allowed to give baths to children at the center. This confirmed in my mind that I was not under any suspicion, and that Hilda and management likely had some twisted agenda or plan.

This became even more apparent to me when, upon my returning to work on Friday, January 29; after two days off, I was ordered to surrender my building key and immediately leave the worksite. Before I could punch in on this day, Claudia intercepted me in the office and led me into a meeting room, where she had another administrative staff member as a witness to our conversation. Though she declined to elaborate; Claudia said that there was a major 'problem' concerning me, and that I needed to report back to the building on Monday, February 1; for a meeting with my union representative, Mack Sterling present. Whatever management had been planning in regards to the bathing issue, it seemed as though this time I had gotten a little too close to the truth.

I had also continued with my whistle-blowing activities. In addition to reports that I made on January 6 and 25, to disclose discriminatory behavior toward me, I had also reported Hilda to management yet again for a new incident on Wednesday, January 20. This particular incident involved Hilda placing a car seat containing a 3-month old baby high up onto a changing table, although the infant had not been strapped into the car seat. At the center, the rule was that infants must be securely strapped whenever placed in a car seat, even if that car seat had been placed on the ground and there was no chance of the infant potentially falling. I was greatly disturbed to learn that Hilda had not taken this most basic safety measure before leaving the car seat and the infant up on the high table. Fortunately I noticed the infant struggling and trying to move about shortly after Hilda had left the room. I shudder to think what grave harm could have befallen this helpless infant as a result of Hilda's serious negligence, which was also witnessed by a child care volunteer. As I had been previously instructed, I submitted a write up on this incident to Children's Services Manager, Candy Rollins. In addition, I also mailed a copy of my report to the DHS. At any rate, my reporting likely caused me to remain a problem in the eyes of the management team.

On Monday, February 1, 2010 at 1:00 p.m.; exactly one week after I reported discrimination to the center's management; Mack and I sat down in a meeting room with the HR Director, Claudia Cahill. Getting straight to the point, Claudia proceeded to inform us that my employment at the center was now being terminated, effective immediately. Adding insult to injury, Claudia proceeded to make the following remarks to me during this meeting:

There are a lot of people employed here, Sumi, who work hard to make this a positive place and focus on being positive. You are the one person, Sumi, who does not do anything to be positive or to make this a positive place. You, Sumi, have turned this into a hostile working environment. You have destroyed relationships here at the workplace.

Following these statements, Claudia proceeded to strongly warn me that I was no longer welcome at the worksite. In making the termination official, Claudia handed Mack and me a written notice of the alleged reasons for my termination. Rather strangely, the termination notice did not list any specific incident or incidents over which I was now being fired. Instead, it merely listed three different company policies, while not specifying at all what I had allegedly done to violate each or any of those policies. I had also not been issued a final written warning leading up to this termination, as is usually a standard procedure.

On this occasion, Mack was supportive and immediately said to me "We are naturally going to file a grievance appealing this decision, correct Sumi?" Of course I said yes in response, and Mack told Claudia that the employee union would file a grievance on my behalf; alleging that the center had violated its contract with the employee union by firing me with the clear absence of 'just cause' for doing so. Following this brief discussion, Claudia rudely ordered me to leave the center that I loved and to never show my face there again.

While I proceeded to comply and leave the building as it snowed, I knew that this fight wasn't over. I decided right then that I was going to fight back with the deadliest weapon of all... a good lawyer!

Chapter Ten

AFTERMATH OF MY TERMINATION

"There are many different aspects involved in the aftermath of my termination. In explaining these to the best of my ability, I have divided them up into four separate phases all contained in this one chapter."

PHASE ONE: HUMAN RIGHTS CHARGE, RESPONSE AND REBUTTAL

Along with the increasingly negative occurrences which I experienced at the center in January 2010, there was one major victory that I have yet to disclose. On Thursday January 14, I had received word that the DHR decided to draft a "Charge of Discrimination" for me against the center. This was indeed a significant victory, as it opened the door to taking legal action and possibly suing my employer. It was also a huge relief and strong validation that my hard work in documenting everything had finally begun to pay off. I was informed about this over the phone by a Human Rights Enforcement Officer, and was told that I would need to stop by the DHR building in person to have the actual charge signed and notarized. Following my termination of February 1, I spoke again with the same Human Rights Enforcement Officer and he drafted an amended charge of discrimination for me against the center, this one to specifically include my termination as part of the discrimination pattern against me. On Friday, February 5, 2010, I traveled to the DHR building again and had the new charge signed and notarized. After six months of waiting and suffering at work, I had *finally* achieved my objective!

However, I would soon learn that this was merely the first of many legal steps to come. Upon speaking with various lawyers, I began to better understand exactly what the DHR's role would be in this complicated process. Upon receiving my charge of discrimination, the center would now be given an opportunity to put together an official response of their own. Once this step was completed, the DHR would mail me a copy of the center's response. Upon receiving this copy, I would then be given another 30 days to put together a rebuttal statement to answer the center's initial response. Once my rebuttal had been submitted, the DHR would assign one sole investigator to look over all of the evidence and eventually issue a ruling. During this lengthy investigation process, which could take a full year or longer, the DHR would be acting only as a neutral party between the two sides. Also during this time, it was likely that the DHR would ask both parties, meaning the center and me, if we were willing to sit down and engage in mediation.

When and if mediation did not work, the final verdict from the DHR would depend on whether or not I had been able to establish what was known as "Probable Cause" for having experienced discrimination. If the DHR concluded that I had indeed established "Probable Cause" in my case, then that would be the greatest victory for me at the end of the day. From my interactions with legal professionals; I had learned that a finding of "Probable Cause," along with a "Right to Sue" letter from DHR, would provide the ammunition necessary to defeat the center in court. I had also learned that if the center still opted not to settle with me at that point, I would clearly have the upper hand in the impending courtroom battle. It was most important to realize, however, that this would be quite a lengthy process. Our lawyers also informed us that it was certainly not an easy task to establish "Probable Cause" in such cases.

This point was driven home most strongly in early March 2010, when I received a 15-page official response in the mail from the center. I remember how angry and intimidated I felt upon reading through their response, as I had never before seen so many negative statements made about me in my entire life. We jokingly referred to it as the "Sumi is a Monster" report! Intimidated as I was, I took a lot of time to read over the entire document with my father. I'm happy to say that at a second glance, I slowly began to notice all the holes in the center's report.

Basically, the center was attempting to argue that I had allegedly been an insubordinate and hostile employee, specifically through my having made many supposedly frivolous complaints about my immediate supervisor, Hilda Hullickson. The center argued that it was really my deteriorating job performance which had led to my termination, instead of any forms of discrimination or retaliation. In trying to make their weak case, the center had listed several incidents which occurred over the course of my employment, where I had either received minor discipline or minor discipline was attempted against me.

Over the next 30 days, my father and I carefully put together a whopping 25-page rebuttal statement in answer to the center's 15-page response. Unbelievable as it may seem, we soon came to learn from the center's report that Claudia Cahill, the HR Director who had fired me, had apparently been a former investigator for the DHR! The center meagerly tried to use this shocking fact as leverage in their overall argument, alleging that it was 'dubious' to believe that someone with Claudia's background in Human Rights would have allowed such atrocious conduct by the center to occur. We countered this argument by making the following important points in our rebuttal statement:

The fact that Ms. Cahill investigated numerous claims of discrimination and retaliation during her tenure with DHR does not qualify her as someone who can create an environment where these things don't happen and it does not qualify her to be able to resolve these things when they are happening.

For someone to be effective in this role the person will need to have a different set of qualifications and experience – she will need to be experienced and effective in providing employee guidance, effective coaching, appropriate and timely training, follow-up, yearly performance reviews and personal improvement plans if deemed necessary, conflict resolution, creating a professional environment where employees do not feel harassed, etc. I regret to report to the State Department that Ms. Cahill tragically fell short in all of these critical areas. This is clearly evidenced by the simple fact that, if Ms. Cahill was a very experienced HR Manager, many of these issues would have likely been resolved a long time ago.

In this eloquent manner, we went on to counter every last point made by the center and their lawyer in their "Sumi Is A Monster" report. Although it would prove to be a time consuming project, it was also extremely rewarding to be able to provide a genuine rebuttal and effectively explain to DHR what had really occurred. The following are several key points that we had raised in our lengthy rebuttal statement to DHR:

To counter the center's claims that I was an overall bad employee with a deteriorating job performance:

we cited my status as being "Volunteer of the Year" from 2006 - 2007, as well as my two glowing performance reviews (in 2007 and 2008) and my "Dedication Award" (in August 2009)… most of which I had received, ironically, from Hilda herself! We also repeatedly made mention of the outstanding fact that I had asked for, but had never received, an annual performance review for the year 2009.

I had politely asked management for a 2009 performance review in my letter of January 6 to the Children's Services Manager. In fact, to my knowledge, I was the only child care provider at the center who DID NOT receive a performance review for the year 2009. If I had, hypothetically, been declining in my job performance as the center alleges, then I should have been given a yearly performance review along with a fair opportunity to make corrections and improve... just as all the other employees were given in 2009. Instead, the only official feedback I received in 2009 was the glowing Dedication Award in August from then supervisor Hilda, which proudly boasted, "In Recognition Of Your Dedication To The Children And Always Looking Out For Their Well Being."

To counter the center's claims that my many reports about Hilda Hullickson's mistreatment of children were 'frivolous':

we submitted a long list of documented eyewitnesses, along with their contact info, who had also observed similar; if not the very same, negative incidents involving Hilda.

This is really where all of my prior documentation came in so handy. Once my reports could be verified by other eyewitnesses, it would be clear for DHR to see that I was fired as retaliation for making honest and genuine reports.

In their response to my charge of discrimination, the center remarkably admitted that

Hilda had made public statements at the workplace similar to the one I've repeatedly quoted, i.e., when Hilda bitterly stated to female employees in my presence, "You know how men are, they can never ask for help!"

Following the center's acknowledgment of this key fact, we submitted the following statements in my rebuttal report:

To summarize, the comment about "men" made by Ms. Hullickson was hardly a casual comment as the center contends, especially given her self-expressed emotional state of mind and her earlier negative remarks to me about another former dark skinned male employee. It was clear that because of the allegedly "horrible" treatment received by Ms. Hullickson from her ex-boyfriend/male roommate over a period of one month, her bitterly spoken, emotional comment about "men" was much more substantial in exposing a growing personal bias. This revealing evidence obtained from Ms. Hullickson's voluntary disclosures; along with Ms. Hullickson's well documented, long term differential treatment towards me, the only man on the PM shift, directly provides the State Department with a smoking gun and 'Probable Cause' for gender discrimination.

I finalized my rebuttal statement in early April 2010 and our lawyer put together a cover page and officially mailed it to the DHR. Within a few weeks, I received an invitation in the mail from DHR, asking me if I was willing to engage in organized mediation with the center. Although I agreed to cooperate, the center and their attorney declined to take part in any meeting. Before long, I was informed by mail that my case had been assigned to a DHR investigator. I also learned that in the event that the DHR investigator was to ultimately conclude that there was not sufficient evidence to establish "Probable Cause," I could then appeal that finding for additional review to the EEOC. After all our hard work, I would now have to sit back and let the investigator begin her lengthy review.

PHASE TWO: EMPLOYEE UNION GRIEVANCE

As we would soon come to learn from our conversations with several lawyers, following through with the grievance filed by my employee union was an essential first step toward taking legal action against the center. As various lawyers explained to us, the courts would not even consider my case until I had first exhausted all avenues of appeal offered through my employee union. As much as I did not wish to work any further with the likes of Mack Sterling and Lakisha Williams, it appeared as though I did not have any choice in the matter. While I wanted to file a motion declaring that I had been suffering from 'inefficient representation' from my union members, my lawyers said I would not have grounds to do so, as long as the union had filed a grievance following my termination... which of course Mack had immediately done on February 1.

As my lawyers would soon explain to us, there was another excellent reason for me to stick with my union grievance. If the union believed that my termination was indeed wrongful, their review committee could ultimately decide to move my grievance onto a critical next phase called "arbitration." Arbitration, our lawyers explained, would consist of legal hearings in which I would be represented by a lawyer belonging to my employee union. On the positive side, I would not have to pay anything for this free representation, whether I lost or even if I prevailed. And if I finally did succeed in arbitration, I could and would actually be awarded back my former job by the employee union! Should this occur, our lawyers explained, it would serve as a tremendous humiliation and black eye to the center's management team. It would be so humiliating, our lawyers contended, that the center may opt to give me a considerable financial settlement to prevent me from walking back into the workplace. "If the union continues to support you, Sumi, that could give us a big piece of leverage at the end of the day," is what I understood from legal professionals.

Seeing the truth in these statements, I reluctantly continued to work with my employee union. However, this process would continue to prove rather aggravating for me, as I would have to endure another meeting with Claudia spewing her same old attitude and approach.

PHASE THREE: FINDING AN APPROPRIATE EMPLOYMENT LAW ATTORNEY

Following a two-week bout in bed with depression, I began to search online for an appropriate employment law attorney. Fortunately now that I was unemployed, I had all the time in the world to research potential lawyers and read about them online. By using the search engines, Yahoo and Google, I entered keywords such as "Best Discrimination Lawyers in my state"; and readily began my journey to find one.

In fact during the early morning hours of Monday, February 15, 2010, I sent out introductory emails to fifteen different lawyers in the area. At this point, I had learned that mentioning my DHR charge would make me a more attractive client to potentially interested law firms.

Fortunately, this appeared to be the case. As it turned out, I received prompt replies from three or four of the fifteen different attorneys I had contacted. Within days my dad and I had multiple lawyer appointments to attend. Two of these appointments occurred on the late afternoon/early evening of Friday, February 26, 2010. The first of these appointments resulted in our meeting with a first class jerk of a lawyer. However, although it was not a good meeting, I was able to obtain some useful information even from this otherwise negative encounter.

Fortunately the second appointment that same evening appeared to hold significant promise for the future. This meeting consisted of my father and I becoming acquainted with the founding partner of a prominent law firm and his much younger, junior attorney. The older man, who I'd read had over 40 years of experience and was licensed in two states; appeared to be about my father's age, in his early 60s. The younger man, coincidentally;

appeared to be much closer to my age, somewhere in his upper 20s to mid 30s.

Our initial meeting with this interesting duo ended up lasting for close to two hours. During this time, we obtained much of the information I have listed in the other phases of this chapter concerning the DHR and my good old employee union. In this meeting we were able to describe everything that had happened thus far in my case to these legal professionals. Unlike our earlier encounter, these gentlemen appeared rather affable and seemed interested in taking my case. In fact by the end of the meeting that night, they had gone ahead and offered to do so!

WHAT I LEARNED WHILE SEARCHING FOR EMPLOYMENT LAW LAWYERS

As was clearly evidenced in my hotel workplace scenario, personal connections are by far the best way to go while searching to find an attorney. Therefore, consult everyone you know personally who may already know of a good employment law attorney.

If left to searching randomly, read up carefully on their lawyer ratings online and Google search/investigate them very well in advance before retaining. Have a trusted and/or legally educated friend/family member read over the retainer agreement before signing. Even after signing, always keep your guard up and know that even the ones with fantastic reputations within the community can still rip you off! Avoid ones who have smaller offices and/or appear to work solo, unless they have been referred by someone you know.

Unless lucky or well-connected in the legal community, prepare for a long and frustrating process of searching, and for potentially dealing with many lawyers who are just looking to pocket your money. Favor those who will not charge you an arm and a leg for a first consultation appointment, and those who may consider a contingency option... although relatively few good ones may readily consider the latter without favorable case circumstances such as a charge and/or probable cause finding from the DHR, or smoking gun evidence, etc.

You may encounter attorneys who immediately come across as being loud, brash, fast-talking, intimidating and aggressive. There are some who will speak to you during normal conversation as though they are grilling you on the witness stand in the courtroom! I personally encountered two such attorneys during my frustrating search. Though lawyers such as these may indeed be well-skilled in their line of work, you may find it difficult to simply converse with them without feeling you are being attacked. I would recommend avoiding the aggressive, fast-talkers; as they are more likely to be combative with you and to lead you away from your best interests. Remember, fast-talking people in general often have their own selfish agendas and could ultimately be more likely to try to talk you out of your cash.

WHAT I LEARNED FROM MEETINGS WITH EMPLOYMENT LAW LAWYERS

What you think might be recoverable damages may not actually be recoverable for a wrongful termination case, even if it is based on illegal retaliation or unlawful discrimination. It seems that damages depend on and vary widely based on what an individual has lost monetarily, as per their particular level of income, length of inability to find new employment with similar income level, total number of employees at the workplace they were fired from, etc. There is no guarantee of what damages will be recoverable. Sometimes the more employees there were at the workplace and/or the higher an individual's income was, might lead to more possible damages. Psychological trauma, if a therapist is willing to testify to it; and defamation of character can have potential for establishing higher damages. I was most shocked to learn that prior to my being fired and losing my source of income, I had apparently not suffered any real 'damages' under the law; in spite of all the harassment, stress, worry and nightmares I had experienced over the years. From my experience; damages in the legal system, it appeared, mainly referred to financial losses instead of genuine and prolonged human suffering.

If a discrimination case such as mine goes to court for trial, I would want a federal-jury-trial, as opposed to a state-jury-trial

It is almost essential to go through the DHR processes; from first filling out an EDQ to obtaining a Charge of Discrimination and eventually all the way to achieving a finding of "Probable Cause"; in order for any good employment law firm to take on your discrimination case and to possibly do so on a preferred contingency basis, meaning you do not pay anything until you have received a settlement. A finding of "Probable Cause" by the DHR is very powerful ammunition for the plaintiff, you, going into a discrimination case.

If you are part of an employee union, it is important that you first exhaust all potential remedies offered by your union before trying to proceed with litigation.

Once you have retained an attorney there is one thing you must remain keenly aware of. If you are on an hourly agreement, you will be billed by the law firm for any and every single time you send your lawyer an email, a phone message or any other form of correspondence in which you seek his or her legal advice. It doesn't matter if it's a one line email or a ten second phone call. You will likely be billed and you must never forget that!

PHASE FOUR: DEMAND LETTER TO THE CENTER

What I learned from my interactions with several legal professionals is that it would be more beneficial to try and get the center cornered into offering me a financial settlement, without having to go into litigation, or an actual courtroom battle. After some lengthy discussions with the employment law firm described above, where we discussed things with the 2-lawyer team, we felt some confidence in the two lawyers' skills and experience to effectively persuade the center's lawyers to settle. Based on these initial interactions and based on our fairly extensive experiences from the lawyer-search process we finally decided to retain this law firm with the two interesting gentlemen in March 2010.

Along with assisting and advising us in regard to pending matters concerning the DHR and the employee union, our new lawyers began the process of representation by sending an introductory letter to the center's attorney. This letter, sent by email and U.S. mail in early March 2010, was intended to simply inform the center that I was now represented by this particular law firm in all matters concerning my recent termination.

Having done so, our lawyers next began the process of constructing a lengthy and forceful 'Demand Letter,' to send to the center as well. The purpose of this letter was to detail my many legal claims against the center, and to make them keenly aware of the impending litigation if they opted not to settle with me. The younger lawyer was to do most of the actual work in regard to my case, while the founding partner of the firm would check in with him and oversee the entire process.

At first I felt somewhat concerned about working with the junior attorney, as I feared that his honest lack of experience might negatively impact my case. But as it turned out, in this situation, the exact opposite proved to be true! I soon came to learn that he was sharp as a whip and exceptionally skilled in the law. Also being younger and relatively new to the legal profession, he seemed extremely sincere and eager to do the best possible job.

He sure as heck did! Over time, my lawyer put together an outstanding 26-page draft-demand letter. The demand letter highlighted my claims for gender discrimination, race and national origin discrimination and whistleblower retaliation; it also offered a timely and confidential end to this legal matter without having to resort to full litigation.

Below is a highly summarized version of what all was said in depth in the letter:

This termination was the culmination of several years' worth of misconduct by the center and its employee directed at Mr. Mukherjee. This misconduct included, most prominently, a pattern of disparate, discriminatory and vindictive treatment by his direct supervisor, Hilda Hullickson. As will be set forth below, Ms. Hullickson's malfeasance included discrimination against Mr. Mukherjee because of his gender, race, national origin, and his whistle-blowing activities. This discrimination largely took the form of repeated attempts to discipline Mr. Mukherjee for supposed "misconduct", for missteps that were either trivial or frivolous or both. Notably none of Mr. Mukherjee's coworkers, who were almost exclusively white females, received discipline for engaging in precisely the same activities and performing work at a lower overall level than Mr. Mukherjee. Mr. Mukherjee complained to upper management on numerous occasions and initiated several union grievances about the ongoing discrimination and harassment, but this egregious abuse continued unabated.

In the end, the center fully condoned and participated in Ms. Hullickson's efforts to discipline and finally terminate Mr. Mukherjee. From the facts presented above, there can be no doubt that in taking these actions, Ms. Hullickson was at least partially motivated by a desire to get back at, and ultimately get rid of, an employee who was conscientious about reporting her misconduct to her superiors and to the appropriate state agencies. In light of the timing of her attempts to discipline, and ultimately discharge Mr. Mukherjee in proximity to his complaints to the center's management and reports to state agencies, and the trivial and/or frivolous nature of the offenses which supposedly formed the basis for Mr. Mukherjee's termination, strong inferential evidence shows that these actions were illegal retaliation.

Aside from the gender discrimination and whistleblower retaliation claims, for which there was ample evidence, my lawyers also strongly suspected the presence of discrimination against me based on my race and national origin. They suspected this because as it turned out I was the only individual in the entire organization, including among all administrative and family services staff members at the center, of East Indian descent. Also during my time as a child care volunteer between 2006-2007; Hilda had made negative statements during a conversation with me about another dark-skinned, male employee who ended up leaving the center just when I was being hired on as a paid employee. This other man had played a significant role in encouraging me to apply for a job at the center; I remember feeling uneasy at the inappropriate remarks that Hilda had made to me about this gentleman and what she perceived to be his alleged promiscuous sexual history.

We got a chance to review the draft demand letter prepared by the lawyers and provided several useful comments and/or suggestions. My lawyers then finalized the lengthy demand letter and mailed it to the center's attorneys on Monday, April 19, 2010. As part of the letter's strong legal dialogue, my lawyers had given the center 20 days from receipt of this letter, until May 10, 2010, to engage in productive settlement discussions or take the risk of us moving right along to litigation.

But after the passage of the next 20 days, there was still no response from the center. However, this was not to suggest for a second that the center didn't have their own plans figured out. In short time, I would soon become aware of the strategic move that they were plotting to make.

Chapter Eleven

THE SEARCH FOR A COOPERATIVE WITNESS

"All that is necessary for the triumph of evil is that good people do nothing." **(Edmund Burke)**

In the months following my wrongful termination from the center, I had been properly deemed eligible to receive appropriate unemployment benefits. But as it turned out, my ex-employer now went on to challenge my eligibility to continue to receive such payments. Incredibly, the organization now falsely alleged that I had supposedly committed 'employment misconduct' during my three years as a child care provider. I was soon informed by my lawyer that this vindictive action would result in an over-the-phone hearing with an unemployment law judge, during which I would have to convince the Judge that I had not committed any misconduct. Although employers typically make such assertions simply because they do not wish to pay benefits to people they have fired, the center had an additional motive behind their decision in my unique case. If I were to be found guilty of committing employment misconduct, such a verdict by a judge could greatly impair my ability to pursue any further legal claims.

Just as the center had done in their response to my DHR charge of discrimination, it appeared as though they would again attempt to portray me at this hearing as having been an insubordinate employee who made false and frivolous complaints concerning the conduct of Hilda Hullickson. Based on discussions with my lawyer, we needed to find eyewitnesses who would be willing to testify at this hearing about the validity of my complaints.

Not wishing to leave any stone unturned, I decided to conduct my search for eyewitnesses by going all the way back to my very first write-up on Hilda, from the end of April 2008. This was the first such incident that I had observed, in which Hilda had shoved a four-year-old boy to the floor of the dining room, causing him to fall right at my feet and right at the feet of a brand new volunteer. Upon reviewing my actual write up from that incident, which I had wisely saved in my computer; I was able to recall the exact observations of the volunteer eyewitness; whom I will call Sheila.

In the paperwork for this first write- up, Sheila had made several statements concerning the misconduct she had observed by Hilda. I recalled how Sheila had felt genuinely disturbed by the incident, specifically having shared with me her concern that the child could have hit his head when he fell. I figured she would likely remember it now, even two years later, as it had occurred on her very first night as a child care volunteer. Though I wasn't sure whether Sheila was still a current volunteer, I was able to obtain her email address by contacting her place of employment; which I happened to recall by chance. Having done so, I then sent Sheila a letter through email explaining my situation to her and politely requesting her assistance.

As it turned out, Sheila declined to respond to my letter in any way. Although I felt let down and disappointed, there wasn't much more that I could do about it. Now if the hearing I was preparing for had been part of an actual trial, then my lawyer could have subpoenaed Sheila and thus forced her to appear and testify truthfully under oath. Because an unemployment benefits hearing is something different than a full-blown trial, it was decided not to subpoena anyone who did not voluntarily choose to testify or become involved in this matter. Since this entire hearing would be conducted over the telephone, my lawyer would not have the usual opportunity to cross examine a reluctant witness in an effective face to face manner, if a witness whom we subpoenaed opted to not tell the truth.

Unfortunately, this was an outcome that I would soon become all too familiar with. Following my attempt to contact Sheila, I proceeded to reach out to another young woman whom I will call Debbie. Debbie was the former PM shift supervisor at the center, prior to Hilda's arrival. According to Mary Monahan, Debbie and Mary had both witnessed behaviors by Hilda during the very first weeks of Hilda's employment at the center, which they had both agreed qualified as being at least 'borderline abusive' conduct toward the children. After much work and effort on my behalf, I was able to obtain Debbie's new home address in another state and also sent her a lengthy letter politely requesting her assistance.

In Debbie's case, she responded to my letter with an email reply, in which she surprisingly claimed to not recall any significant issues with Hilda's behavior toward the children. Unsure of what to think, I then proceeded to contact Mary Monahan just to confirm what she had previously told me. And once again, Mary confirmed for me that she firmly remembered Debbie admitting to her that Debbie had observed inappropriate behaviors toward children by Hilda. However when I sent Debbie a second, very polite letter mentioning some of the things that Mary remembered, Debbie failed to respond to me at all. Although I was again disappointed by the reaction of this eyewitness, I saved Debbie's contact info for the day that my case went to court.

In spite of these first two setbacks concerning eyewitnesses, I certainly had high hopes when I went on to approach my longtime personal friend and professional adviser, Connie Cooper. Although Connie had never witnessed any misconduct by Hilda at the center where I had worked, it was decided by our team that she could potentially be a good witness for this hearing. After all, Connie could testify about how she had observed my excellent conduct toward children at her place of employment. She could also verify that I had sought out her professional advice throughout the years regarding troubles at the center.

But to my great shock and dismay, my good friend and mentor refused to even consider the idea of being involved in this matter. "Oh Sumi, I just cannot afford to get involved in this situation!" Connie sharply said to me in a panicked tone. "I have the same employee union as you do at your center, and I don't want to take any chance at all with my job and my livelihood."

As disappointing as this third setback was, even it soon paled in comparison to my fourth eyewitness disaster. This one involved the ex-receptionist who had made many revealing statements to me about the HR Director, Claudia Cahill; on July 15, 2009. As in two of the previous cases, I sent the ex-receptionist a very detailed, polite letter through email requesting her assistance.

Again to my great disappointment, the ex-receptionist responded but now went on to completely change her tune and denied having given me much of the information which she had provided! Though reading her response was quite aggravating, it still had potential value should it end up in a court of law. Whether she realized it or not, the ex-receptionist had at least admitted to engaging in the phone conversation with me on July 15, 2009. Moreover she had also admitted to having suggested to me; in some way, shape or form; that I should indeed investigate Claudia's credentials. If this ex-receptionist were to be cross-examined someday by my lawyer in court, I believe that a skilled attorney would get the truth out of her. Angry and frustrated as I felt at the moment, I made sure that I saved this email.

While this outcome was certainly disappointing, I never could have predicted what the ex-receptionist was about to do next. Unbelievably, this same individual, who had repeatedly stated that she did not wish to become involved; then went on to contact Claudia Cahill and provided Claudia with the letter that I had sent requesting her to testify! In doing so, the ex-receptionist claimed that she wanted Claudia to know that she had not said any negative things to me about Claudia's job performance. I was sickened to see that the ex-receptionist changed her stance so bluntly over things she had openly told me. Essentially, she was denying that she had ever told me any of those things, and it seemed to me that she was simply covering up for herself.

Needless to say, I felt profoundly discouraged as this process forced me to observe the more cowardly, selfish and deceitful sides of human nature. Just as Edmund Burke had famously stated, "All that is necessary for the triumph of evil is that good men, and/or good women, do nothing." Sadly, I felt I was beginning to see just how true his statement had been.

However, fortunately there were a couple of sincere people and key eyewitnesses who DID find the courage to speak out truthfully on my behalf... and on behalf of the children at the center. Mary Monahan, God bless her, wholeheartedly agreed to talk with my lawyer and to participate in my unemployment benefits hearing.

Along with providing this direct support from herself, Mary even went the extra mile and informed me of the recent emergence of a brand new, smoking gun eyewitness at the center.

On the morning of Thursday, April 29, 2010 at 6:41 a.m., I received the following revealing email from Mary:

> Hi Sumi,
>
> I was really glad to talk to your lawyer. I hope that at some point something turns the center around. Do you remember Helen Johnson, the volunteer that usually worked on

Wednesdays? She met with Executive Director Karen Patrick around the first part of March. She was upset about some staff treatment of children. She also backed you up at that meeting. She told Karen Patrick there were facts to support you about Hilda. Karen Patrick asked if she would be willing to talk to Claudia, but I'm not sure if she did speak with Claudia yet. I think it might be important that your lawyer knows that Karen Patrick has been personally told these allegations are true.

Your friend,

Mary

Mary's information provided me the big break I had been searching for. This meant that in addition to all the eyewitnesses who had observed Hilda mistreating children over the years, now a brand new one had come forward even after they got rid of me! Not only had Helen confirmed that Hilda's mistreatment of the children continues, she specifically told Karen Patrick that my concerns about Hilda were true. The question remaining now was why Karen Patrick had redirected Helen to go speak with Claudia Cahill, of all people, instead of Karen handling the matter herself as the center's Executive Director? It appeared as though Claudia Cahill had forcefully taken control of that place.

As I would soon come to learn via Mary; this volunteer, Helen, not unlike many of the others, was feeling reluctant to get further involved in this matter. Regardless, my lawyer felt Helen's testimony was so crucial to my case that he requested the judge to subpoena her and demand that she speak at my hearing.

But would Helen actually tell the truth when and if she was ordered to speak? The answer would come in a one of a kind unique hearing to take place in May.

Chapter Twelve

MINI-TRIAL OF UNEMPLOYMENT BENEFITS HEARING

"The burden of proof in this hearing falls on the center and its lawyer. Speaking in sports lingo, we will enter this battle ahead by two touchdowns." **Statement made to me by my lawyer, in helping me to understand my position going into the benefits hearing.**

As the month of May slowly passed by, my lawyer did an excellent job in preparing me for the mini-trial of our unemployment benefits hearing. This hearing would be unique in nature, he explained, as it would all be conducted over the telephone without any visual contact with the other participants. He also explained that unlike at an actual courtroom trial or litigation, the usual 'rules of evidence' would not apply at this hearing. Although a high burden of proof would fall squarely on the shoulders of my ex-employer, I would still have to effectively convey my sincerity to the judge in sharp contrast to damning testimony from the top authority figures at the center. My lawyer was quick to point out that out of the twenty or so unemployment cases which he had successfully handled, never before had he seen four levels of management, the Executive Director; the HR Director; the Children's Services Manager; and the former supervisor, all scheduled to appear together to represent the employer. As it turned out Children's Services Manager, Candy Rollins, was laid off in the aftermath of my termination and shortly before the hearing took place; I was informed about this on May 20, 2010, by Mary Monahan.

Because of my DHR charge, my threatening demand letter and the implications of further legal action on my behalf; the center was doing everything in their power to make all of this go away. Once again, if I were to be found guilty of having committed employment misconduct, such a verdict by a judge could greatly impair my ability to pursue any further legal claims.

As for the hearing itself; my lawyer instructed me to speak in a clear, loud, and confident tone of voice when testifying and to always say 'Yes, Your Honor' politely when addressing the judge. He also advised me to provide answers that were brief and right to the point, and to not elaborate beyond that or end up going off on a tangent. "Unemployment judges tend to become irritated if an individual's testimony deviates from the specific focus of this particular hearing," my lawyer explained. In other words, I would have to resist the temptation to directly point an accusing finger at Hilda, Claudia or to boldly place blame on my ex-employer for all that they had done wrong. I had to accept that this hearing was about me and my conduct, and not intended to focus on my ex-employer's negative actions. Along with advising me to remain calm and keep my emotions in check, my lawyer also said that it is appropriate at these hearings to honestly convey to the judge that I have felt 'frustrated' with how I was being treated. "To say that you have felt 'frustrated' is a very acceptable and appropriate word to use in these kind of hearings," my lawyer explained.

As it turned out, my unusual unemployment benefits mini-trial resulted in over-the-phone hearings with a judge over a span of three separate days in the spring and summer of 2010: Wednesday, May 26; Thursday, June 17; and Friday, July 9. During these hearings, the organization presented several incidents that occurred over the course of my employment which had resulted

Sumi Mukherjee

in either minor discipline or attempts at minor discipline being imposed against me.

However my ex-employer's strongest allegation of employment misconduct on my behalf was once again their strange, fabricated contention that I was supposedly insubordinate by way of making *false and frivolous* reports to the center management and board of directors about Hilda Hullickson. They also alleged that I was *hostile and uncooperative* during numerous interactions with management. To verify that my many complaints about Hilda were not frivolous; I requested fellow eyewitnesses, Mary Monahan and Helen Johnson, to testify on my behalf.

Mary, the former supervisor, shift leader and respected ten-year employee of the organization; testified truthfully on Wednesday, May 26, 2010, to previously witnessing Hilda slam a small toddler into a chair and witnessing Hilda's aggressiveness toward another child during a mealtime. Helen, the long-term child care volunteer with the organization for 17 years and my new 'smoking gun' eyewitness; also testified truthfully on May 26 to recently witnessing Hilda's 'anger issues' and 'enraged behavior' toward children, specifically observed during mealtimes as well. In addition to this testimony about Hilda's negative behaviors, Mary also testified truthfully about how I had always been an excellent employee who took special care to address the children's needs and concerns.

In desperately attempting to counter this damning testimony and to make their weak case for the judge; the HR Director, Claudia Cahill; testified at great length on Thursday, June 17, 2010; that she believed I had supposedly presented some form of 'serious threat to the safety of the children at the center', although she had no documentation whatsoever to back up her slandering allegations. In doing so, Claudia spoke about how she had supposedly called the local police following my termination, and had expressed her concerns to them about my potential to return

90

to the worksite and harm her and the children! Claudia also claimed, just as she had during a union grievance hearing on March 8 that members on the center's Board of Directors were supposedly concerned about the safety of the children who were around me. Executive Director Karen Patrick also testified on Friday, July 9, 2010, that she believed I had supposedly behaved in an 'erratic and obsessive' manner; although there was again no documentation whatsoever to back up her claims of this nature.

IT TOOK EVERYTHING I HAD to just sit there and listen as Claudia said things under oath that I believed to be untrue, and made me out to be some kind of terrifying monster. However, my favorite part of the hearing came moments later on Thursday, June 17; when my lawyer got his chance to cross examine the HR Director, Claudia. Piece by piece, question by question, my lawyer tore Claudia apart during his grueling thirty-six minute cross-examination of her. It was very gratifying to observe such a previously headstrong bully like Claudia now squirming to answer the most basic questions concerning my wrongful termination. Cornered time and again by my lawyer, Claudia became quite flustered and even at one point undermined her own credibility in answering a tough question by meagerly pleading, "Well I have only been the HR Director there for a short period of time, so I don't know everything that goes on!"

In short, Claudia balked at questions having to do with why the center had not followed proper disciplinary procedure in giving me both a suspension and a final warning before she abruptly fired me on February 1. Claudia also diminished her credibility further by attempting to use a past minor incident against me, one for which it turned out I had not even received any discipline or oral coaching whatsoever, since management had not deemed it necessary at the time it occurred.

Most importantly, Claudia could not produce evidence of any alleged incidents which the employer claimed had occurred between my having received warnings over two minor incidents on January 8, 2010; and my sudden, unprovoked termination on February 1. The judge clearly appeared confused and irritated at the fact that my former employer could not provide any further examples of discipline and/or alleged 'misconduct' occurring over the month preceding my termination. In fact, Claudia became so rattled by my lawyer that she actually went on to express her frustrations with the judge and to sternly accuse the judge of attempting to 'twist' her words! My lawyer silently flashed two thumbs up at the precise moment when this incident occurred.

And it only got better from there. Moments later, under specific questioning from the employer's attorney, Claudia shockingly revealed that she was no longer employed by the center. Incredibly Claudia now stated that she had 'voluntarily' left her position as HR Director, after a term of less than 16 months, in the aftermath of my dismissal. This led me to believe that Claudia had clearly realized just how badly things were handled in this situation, and had chosen to jump ship before things got worse. In reflection, it appeared as though the ex-receptionist had been correct about Claudia's background.

But perhaps the biggest surprise of all came when my lawyer questioned former supervisor, Hilda Hullickson. In his cross examination on June 17; in sharp contrast to Claudia's earlier testimony, Hilda testified truthfully that I had presented 'no threat to the safety of the children at the center, and that there were 'no significant performance issues' with me leading up to my termination on February 1. ... at this point my lawyer smiled and non-verbally communicated to me his enthusiastic feelings about the possible positive outcome of this hearing. Hilda also admitted to presenting me with a "Dedication Award," while she was my supervisor, in August 2009. The Award specifically stated "In Recognition of Your Dedication To The Children and Always Looking Out For Their Well Being." Hilda also testified that she personally had no role in my termination; while Claudia Cahill and Karen Patrick both testified that they were behind my abrupt departure.

Also in testimony at the hearing on June 17; former HR Director, Claudia, expressed frustration and complained about the fact that I had reported my serious concerns about Hilda's prolonged mistreatment of children to the DHS, and that the DHS had in turn paid the center a visit to investigate. However, in the company's employee handbook, it clearly stated that "All reports to the DHS will be respected and no retaliation shall occur." This employee handbook statement is in direct contrast to Claudia's frustrated attitude about my having approached the DHS in good faith as a mandated reporter.

And also during the final hearing on Friday, July 9, 2010; Executive Director, Karen Patrick, admitted to the judge that volunteer Helen Johnson had met with her on March 1, 2010; and that Helen had voiced serious concerns about three staff members at the center "taking their rage out" on the children. Of the three child care providers whose behavior Helen had reported during this meeting; one was Hilda and another was the long-term abusive employee, Crystal Matthews, for whom Hilda had apparently concealed my maltreatment report on July 17, 2009.

In addition to all of this; Helen had even informed Ms. Patrick, quite specifically according to Ms. Patrick's testimony, that "Sumi's concerns about Hilda Hullickson's mistreatment of children are valid." I really wasn't sure why Ms. Patrick had gone ahead and volunteered this revealing information to us, but at any rate it fully validated my long expressed concerns about Hilda. Why Ms. Patrick had STILL not taken appropriate action to remove Hilda or Crystal, now even after Helen had recently come forward, remained the most baffling mystery of all. I just couldn't understand why these well-documented, long-term abusive employees were being allowed to continue to mistreat our society's most vulnerable children.

I learned from my interactions with the legal professionals that most unemployment benefit hearings concluded over the course of one day and after about one hour of testimony. In my unique case, I did not even get to testify until the third and final day of the hearing; Friday, July 9. During cross-examination by my former employer's team, I kept my cool and answered all their questions in a confident and articulate manner. Most of their inquiries involved asking me for a brief explanation of the several minor incidents the center was now bringing forward.

Most important of all, I DID NOT react with anger or strong emotion when the center's lawyer baited me to do so. In fact, when the attorney questioned me about my personal opinion as to why I had been terminated, I kept my response brief and unspecific by saying something to the effect of, "Well, I could certainly speculate about why I was terminated, but I do not see anything positive or productive that could come from dwelling on it today." While the attorney had likely hoped that I'd go off on a tangent about the conspiracy among the center's top authority figures to get rid of me, I smartly refused to take the bait. Also when she asked me about statements I'd made in my email to the center's former receptionist weeks after my termination, in which I had described Claudia as being the "Cunning and Evil Mastermind" behind everything wrong occurring at the center, I calmly replied to this by saying; "I was expressing my 'frustration' over the entire situation to someone who I thought I could confide in, and I did not intend for those comments to ever be brought to Claudia's attention."

At this point, the judge appeared frustrated and instructed the employer's attorney to stop questioning me about statements I had made in this letter several weeks *after* my dismissal. "These questions have no relevance to this hearing!" the judge said sternly to the employer's attorney, who was then forced to abandon this unnecessary line of questions.

Knowing full well they had a weak case against me, the center's attorney had attempted to use my letter to the ex-receptionist as a supposed example of how I could be such a negative person to work with. From discussions with my lawyer, I had understood that it would likely not be a major issue since the letter had no relevance to this hearing. Fortunately the judge clearly saw right through this lawyer's tactic and directed the center's attorney to pursue a different line of questioning. At any rate, this serves as an excellent reminder that anything one writes and sends out to someone else, could eventually find its way into a court of law.

On a more humorous note, in her earlier testimony on June 17, Claudia had whimpered about how my characterization of her in my letter to the ex-receptionist had hurt her feelings and had come across as being 'a scathing and harsh review'. What I felt like saying at that moment was... so sorry Claudia, but if the shoe fits you gotta wear it; maybe you'll think about it the next time before you bully someone at a workplace.

Finally on Wednesday, July 21, 2010, after an agonizing twelve days of waiting, I received news that I had prevailed in the mini-trial of the unemployment benefits hearing. This was a huge legal victory for a number of reasons. Not only would I no longer collect unemployment payments if I had lost, but I would have also been forced to pay back several thousand dollars in benefits which I had already received. I also knew a defeat would have likely meant that my employee union would subsequently drop the grievance I had filed through them appealing my wrongful termination. My lawyer, meanwhile, was quick to inform the union about my success in the benefits hearing. As it turned out; after receiving no open communication from the union, and what it seemed to me to be dragging their feet for four and a half months, I received great news from my employee union on

Saturday, July 24, 2010. I got a letter in the mail, only three days after receiving the news of my unemployment benefits victory, saying that the union's arbitration review committee had *finally* ruled that my case was indeed fit to 'Proceed To Arbitration!'

Just as validating as the arbitration news, were the judge's written comments in the letter declaring that I remained eligible to receive unemployment benefits. The following are some of my favorite comments that the judge made in his written ruling:

> *Mr. Mukherjee took his job duties seriously and attempted to improve his performance when warned. A preponderance of the evidence does not support a finding that the performance issues that resulted in Mr. Mukherjee's receiving either written or oral warnings during the last several months of his employment, were so serious or significant, even when taken together, to constitute employment misconduct. In any event, the evidence supports a finding that Mr. Mukherjee was discharged as a consequence of his making complaints regarding his immediate supervisor during the last several months of his employment to one or more members of the board and the executive director, Karen Patrick. Mr. Mukherjee was viewed as an antagonistic and insubordinate employee as a result of these complaints.*

Along with validating that I had been a good employee and that I had indeed suffered retaliation for my whistle-blowing activities; the judge also commented on the fact that I had properly followed instructions given to me by management on Tuesday, December 22, 2009; which were to strictly follow the chain of command from then on when reporting any future concerns. On this particular issue, the judge made the following written remarks:

Mr. Mukherjee presented uncontested testimony that following the counseling he received during the middle of December 2009, he stopped making these complaints to others beyond his immediate supervisor's supervisor. Mr. Mukherjee complied with the expectations that were expressed in this counseling. It should also be noted that there were no other reported incidents following the last warnings that Mr. Mukherjee received during the first week of January 2010. Mr. Mukherjee did not receive either a suspension or final warning prior to his discharge. The employment law judge accepts Mr. Mukherjee's testimony that he had no clear understanding or awareness that his job was in any immediate jeopardy despite receiving the warnings in January. While this employer may have felt that it had good business reasons to terminate Mr. Mukherjee's employment, the employment law judge is not persuaded that these reasons rise to the level of employment misconduct as that term is defined above. Mr. Mukherjee is eligible to receive unemployment benefits.

Since that most awful day, December 22, 2009; I had complied wholeheartedly and sent all new concerns only to Hilda's immediate supervisor, Children's Services Manager, Candy Rollins. While I also sent copies of my reports to the DHS, I did not break the chain of command within the organization. I did not bring any more concerns to the Executive Director or Board of Directors. I was gratified that the judge commended me for taking my job duties seriously and politely adhering to the requests made of me by management. Doing the right thing had paid off.

Unfortunately, many good people in my position would have gone ahead and quit their employment, naturally not wanting to subject themselves to even more grief and aggravation. That, specifically, is what some organizations count on in order to thrive and bully their employees. But I didn't take the bait, largely due to good advice I had received from a lawyer my dad and I consulted during a meeting in December 2009. Based on that advice, I continued to be polite and cooperative with management and kept on doing my job correctly, so that if they screwed up and fired me it would be their bad mistake.

With these recent legal victories having strengthened my position, our current lawyer mailed a copy of the judge's decision and comments to my employee union and the DHR. In addition to doing so, we also suggested that he and his boss communicate with the center's attorney once again, to see if their side would be willing to negotiate or possibly consider a settlement option. In spite of my recent successes, the center's lawyer again responded by saying that her client did not wish to discuss settlement options at this time. The battle and the waiting, it seemed, was not quite over with yet.

Chapter Thirteen

EXPLORING NEW OPTIONS AND WAITING ON AN ANSWER FROM DHR

"Perseverance, in the face of many delays and tremendous frustration, is essential if you hope to succeed against a bully employer."

After spending most of the summer consumed with fighting the unemployment benefits battle, I was deeply disappointed to learn that the center was still not willing to settle. In working with our legal team we had the impression that our big victory in the benefits arena; along with my union's subsequent, long overdue decision to move my grievance onto arbitration; would likely corner the center into discussing a settlement plan. And in light of the evidence revealed during the hard fought benefits hearing, it remained a mystery to us why the center had simply refused to back down.

This noncompliance by my ex-employer left us to ponder our legal options. What would we do if the center wasn't intimidated by the prospect of arbitration, or if the DHR failed to return a finding of probable cause? Although our lawyers would still take our case under these dire circumstances, their company had a strict policy against taking cases on a contingency basis. Contingency would mean that we wouldn't have to pay our lawyers a whole lot until and/or unless we finally won a settlement in court.

But without a preferred contingency agreement, our lawyers estimated the legal fees we would pay through lengthy litigation could approach the mark of $100,000! Naturally, we would not be able to afford such prolonged representation. Having our lawyer defend me at the three unemployment hearings alone had cost us $7,000. This law firm also assured us that they would not consider a contingency option even if the DHR did return a much desired finding of probable cause.

While this law firm had put forth a sincere effort to help us, it appeared that our legal system was primarily established to service the rich. Regardless of the merits of my case or the well-being of the center's children, it appeared that we needed big money to secure proper representation. I couldn't help but feel genuine fury toward a system that works in this manner, where employers automatically have the best lawyers while you're left struggling to assert your basic rights. This is why most employers expect those 'little people' who they have wronged to eventually give up and quit... as the vast majority of them unfortunately do. Something in our legal system needs to change to level the playing field in this regard. Perseverance, in the face of many delays, high financial costs and tremendous frustration, appeared to be essential if you hope to succeed against a bully employer.

From the end of July until mid-August 2010, we were back on the road in search of a lawyer again; specifically a good one who might consider taking our case on a contingency basis. By the grace of God and the internet, we were saved at the last moment from signing on with a guy who had received scathing written reviews from his previous clients! The day before we were about to sign on with this lawyer, who had been willing to take our case on a full contingency basis, I happened to look him up on Google and found highly concerning information about him. In light of these shocking revelations, we decided to keep on searching. In all likelihood, we felt as though we had really dodged a bullet. After all our searching, we finally came across one reasonable prospect on Wednesday, August 18, 2010. This individual was a remarkably bright young lady who came across as being outraged at the center's misconduct and possibly interested in taking my case on a contingency basis. We simply crossed our fingers while waiting to hear back from her.

On Friday, October 1, 2010, we were finally able to sit down and meet with the young lady lawyer. While she continued to express a strong interest in taking my case on a contingency basis, she explained that upper management at her law firm was simply not willing to do so. Yet, it appeared that all hope was not lost. She explained that her firm would likely agree to take on my case in the future on a contingency basis, but only after I received a favorable ruling from the DHR.

However, we were certainly not about to slow down in our efforts toward attaining proper representation. During a follow up phone conversation between ourselves and this lawyer on Thursday, October 14, 2010, we were able to discuss some other possibilities of how her law firm might be willing to take on our case, even if by chance the DHR did not come back with a 'Probable Cause' finding. This discussion seemed a lot more promising than the one thirteen days earlier. The attorney provided a possible contingency fee structure in the event of a positive finding by DHR and an alternative fee structure that provided us with some fee certainties to proceed in the event that the DHR did not make a probable cause finding. In other words, even if the DHR did not find a probable cause, we would be able to go forward with this attorney on a plan based on some fees and some contingency approach rather than all fees or all contingency approach.

These options clearly gave us a lot more reasons to remain hopeful. Now even if the DHR did not follow through, in what would be a worst case scenario for us, we knew that we might still have other options to fight the center. Meanwhile, we sent a request through our original lawyer to politely ask my DHR investigator for a status update regarding my case.

But the path to obtaining justice would branch off in several different directions. Along with pursuing my DHR claims, it was time for me to also check in with my good old employee union.

Chapter Fourteen

WAITING PATIENTLY FOR MY EMPLOYEE UNION TO ACT

"We expect this case to be a slam dunk win on our behalf. Your ex-employer has no evidence against you." **Positive comments made to me by my employee union representative, Lakisha Williams, during a meeting at union headquarters in March 2010.**

Along with the several steps I took concerning the DHR, I also continued to maintain communication with my employee union. In fact on Friday, October 15, 2010, I met with senior union representative, Lakisha Williams, to discuss the upcoming arbitration proceedings. It had now been nearly three months since the union had informed me about their decision to pursue arbitration on July 24, and a full seven months since the original termination grievance hearing, with Claudia, in March 2010. But this particular meeting, unlike that horrible one in March, went smoothly and exceptionally well. Lakisha and a union colleague both informed me how they and my ex-employer would soon begin the process of selecting an arbitrator from a list of between five to seven potential people for the job. They explained that each side would get to strike down potential arbitrators from the list that they did not like, until there was just one remaining to work with.

But aside from these technicalities, Lakisha and her colleague repeatedly emphasized what a strong case they felt I had against my ex-employer. Just as she had stated at the end of the original termination grievance hearing on March 8, 2010, Lakisha again said that they fully expected my case to be a 'slam dunk win' on our behalf. Both insisted that my ex-employer, and specifically the former HR Director, Claudia Cahill; had clearly not established 'just cause' in terminating my employment as required in the center's contract with the employee union. Both also emphasized that my ex-employer had 'no evidence against me,' and that this was a battle they felt compelled to fight on my behalf as my employee union. "This thing is bigger than just you, Sumi," Lakisha said to me with confidence on October 15. "This case has larger implications for all of us, and it is a case we really need to fight on principle." They also emphasized the significance and importance that my unemployment benefits victory, along with the judge's specific comments about retaliation, would have during this arbitration hearing. "I have handled a previous case, Sumi, where the worker's victory during his unemployment benefits hearing carried great weight during arbitration and helped him reclaim his job," Lakisha said in an enthusiastic tone.

In better explaining what was next to come, Lakisha said they would first attempt to ask the center if they were willing to engage in 'mediation,' which was a step below actual arbitration and would save the losing side; presumably the center, from having to pay the high costs of an all-out arbitration hearing. Lakisha explained that the arbitration process would likely cost between $3,000 to $5,000 per day for the losing party. Lakisha also said that if my ex-employer were to instead, "remain cocky and still opt for full arbitration," then they would be making a poor decision which would only prove self-defeating for them.

At any rate; I was quite gratified to know that Executive Director, Karen Patrick, now appeared cornered and was left with some tough decisions to make. Lakisha again confirmed that both former HR Director, Claudia Cahill; and former Children's Services Manager, Candy Rollins; were no longer employed at the center.

However, stunningly; she also informed me that former supervisor, Hilda Hullickson; still remained employed there as a child care provider. I found this information to be disheartening and troubling, especially since Mary Monahan and I had both reported Hilda's chronic mistreatment of children to the DHS so many months ago. I was profoundly disappointed in both the center as well as the DHS in this regard. If these two organizations would not look out for the safety of our society's most vulnerable children, then who else could be expected to do so?

In addition to this information, Lakisha also went on to explain that the center had been suffering financially and their new HR Director was currently only able to work three days a week; Mondays, Wednesdays and Fridays. Finally, Lakisha praised me for my continued patience in this ongoing matter, and conceded that this was indeed a very long process. "We need to stop your unemployment payments and get you back into work soon!" Lakisha said to me in an upbeat manner as we both stood up to shake hands. During this meeting, Lakisha also voiced her personal belief that I had likely been treated more harshly by the women in authority at the center, due to my gender as a male. Lakisha concluded the October 15 meeting by saying that she would soon be hearing from the center's new HR Director, and that she would contact me as soon as she had a date set for the hearing.

But as great and validating as all this news was, it was soon balanced once again by the lack of productive action. Soon October turned into November, and November into December... with no action toward arbitration. Although I tried my best to continue to remain patient during this period, I eventually decided at a certain point that further correspondence was essential. I was careful to follow my own advice given earlier in this book; that is to make sure every written correspondence that I send out, especially letters and emails; is written while bearing in mind that it could one day, potentially, be read aloud in a court of law.

Keeping this notion in mind, I sent Lakisha the following email on Monday, November 8, 2010:

Hello Lakisha! I hope you are doing well after the big election.

I just wanted to inquire as to whether you have heard back from the center's new HR Director, regarding arbitration? I'm concerned that if given time, the center will simply continue to delay this process indefinitely.

Thanks and have a good week!

Sumi

Fortunately Lakisha responded to this message in a timely manner, and sent me the following reply later that same morning:

Hi Sumi – I have spoken with the center, and we're still talking about mediation or arbitration, I'll keep you posted, thanks for your patience.

Lakisha

In spite of her timely response, the weeks continued to pass by without my hearing anything new from Lakisha. Though I was beginning to feel a little frustrated inside, I decided to take advantage of the Thanksgiving holiday to send Lakisha a kindly worded email wishing her well on Wednesday, November 24. When this email failed to elicit a response back from Lakisha in another week's time, I then sent her yet another new email, this one on Wednesday, December 1, 2010:

Hello Lakisha and Happy December! It looks like old man winter is finally here for a while. I hope you had a good Thanksgiving, and didn't eat too much turkey or stuffing this year. =)

It occurred to me that today marks exactly ten months since my wrongful termination, on Mon. Feb. 1st. With us fast approaching the new year, I just wanted to inquire and make sure that we won't be passing any statute of limitations in regards to my arbitration? I remain quite concerned that if given more time, the center will continue to delay this process indefinitely. Obviously, they realize what they are up against and are not going to want to do this anytime soon.

Please understand that I am trying my best to remain patient... in fact I think I have more 'patience' than a doctor, HAHA! But seriously, if you can give me some kind of timeline perhaps of how much longer I can expect to wait, then I won't risk bombarding you with my good natured reminders. I am really trying to be patient, but it seems to become more difficult with the ongoing passage of time.

> *Thank you as always for your time and efforts, Lakisha! I hope to hear back from you at your earliest convenience.*
>
> *Sumi*

To this latest message, Lakisha responded promptly, later the same day with the following reply:

> *Hey Sumi – thanks for the holiday wishes and good cheer. Hope you and your family enjoy this precious season!!! Nothing new to report regarding the arbitration, I recognize the lengthiness of this process, and I so much appreciate your patience. Hopefully all this patience won't be in vain – we believe we have a good solid case, and we believe we will prevail in the end. Thanks again Sumi – Holiday wishes and cheer to you and your family.*
>
> *Lakisha*

Although she had responded once again in a timely manner, I was quite irritated and angry at the lack of relevant content in

Lakisha's reply. Once again, I did not know what to make of this employee union, and did not know exactly where this continued delay in the process was coming from. I also began to wonder if perhaps the center was trying to delay this just long enough so that some potential legal time limit may expire. Though I found myself feeling extremely frustrated at this point, I proceeded to send out the following, very carefully thought out email to Lakisha later that same evening; Wednesday, December 1, 2010:

Dear Lakisha,

Thanks so much for responding to me, yet again. It is clear to me that I am not the only one here who has remarkable patience, and please always know that I do understand that you are doing the utmost you can!

Unfortunately, I am still quite confused about what specifically is occurring to delay arbitration at the present moment. It has been over four months since the decision to 'proceed to arbitration' came down in July. At our last meeting on Oct. 15th, you did an excellent job in explaining to me the processes of arbitration vs. mediation, and what all was involved in both. I've come to find there is no substitute for detailed and accurate information.

Today I find myself in the position of needing to ask you again for some detailed and accurate information. Following that last meeting, I was under the impression that we would be hearing back from the center's HR Director within a week or so, and that any actual proceedings, whether arbitration or mediation, would occur sometime after the Nov. 2nd election.

Well, now it's Dec. 1st and still nothing. If you could attempt to answer the following specific questions for me, I would appreciate it more than my words can describe:

1. Is there a statute of limitations on when/how an arbitration proceeding can occur?

2. You mentioned again that this is a 'long process' which requires much patience. Can you give me a ballpark idea, or a timeline, of exactly how much longer this could potentially drag on? On Oct. 15th, you had explained quite well for me how things had worked in other arbitration cases, such as how the verdict in an unemployment benefits hearing can carry much weight in this battle. How does my case compare to other similar cases as far as the waiting time thus far? Does it normally take nearly one year to win back a wrongfully terminated individual's job? If my case is taking longer than average to resolve, why is that happening and what can we do to productively work together to expedite the process?

3. Is the current delay being caused by the center, or is it on behalf of the employee union?

4. If the center simply refuses to get back to you or to cooperate, what can we do to productively work together to expedite the stalling process?

Again, I applaud you for your patience with me and for finding the time in your busy day to correspond. In my extremely difficult position, knowing something is always much more comforting and humane than not having a clue as to what is really going on with my case. This ordeal is causing me much emotional anguish, and I would greatly, tremendously appreciate if you could attempt to directly answer the four questions I have put forth above.

Thank you once again, Lakisha, for your ongoing dedication in pursuing justice properly through the system. You are clearly an asset to your organization, and an inspirational person all around. Thanks again! =)

Sumi

By this point I had grown disgusted with sending these nicey, nice emails and having to kiss up! However, I wanted to take all positive actions to move the case forward and to be cognizant of any statute of limitation issues. I did not want to be faced with any argument later that I had not acted timely. Most importantly, I had to make darn sure that I always came across as very constructive, gentle and polite toward Lakisha. By doing so, nobody could ever come back and question whether or not I had been positive in my behavior. Sharing my frustration, it certainly appeared, was a gift I would have to save for those folks who would someday be reading this book.

And much like before, there would definitely be more frustration ahead. As it turned out, I did not hear back from Lakisha this time for almost the next two weeks. When she did finally respond to my detailed inquiries, it was merely to provide a similar brief message to the ones I'd received before.

But regardless of all this uncertainty, a much bigger question remained. Would I choose to accept my former job back, if I were to prevail in the end?

Chapter Fifteen

BRAND NEW DHR CLAIM AND IMPENDING MEDIATION

"As you may recall from chapter nine, 'physical or mental disability' is a protected class status under the Human Rights Act, just as race, gender, age, and sexual orientation are."

As it turned out, the arrival of the New Year brought with it the progression in my legal case that I had long awaited… and in more ways than just one. On Tuesday, January 4, 2011, I received an email from my union representative, Lakisha Williams. She informed me that the center had finally decided that they would like to engage in the less formal process of mediation, as opposed to them opting for arbitration. I naturally welcomed this news, especially since it appeared consistent with Lakisha's long stated belief that I had a rather strong case against my former employer.

Still, I had no clue about what all was involved in the legal process of mediation. With the actual date of the impending hearing still unscheduled, we met with both our current lawyer as well as the potential contingency lawyer with whom we soon hoped to work. Both of these separate meetings went quite well, as both lawyers relayed very similar information to us about the mediation process. We learned that mediation would involve the center's representatives and I being seated in different rooms, with a selected mediator to go between the rooms and communicate with both sides. My side, of course, would consist of myself and

111

my union representatives. The mediator's role was to try to make both sides doubt the strength of their respective case, so that both sides will feel more compelled to reach a solution in the mediation. Based on what we learned, we understood that I would have more personal input and control over the final outcome during mediation. The issue of me returning to work was discussed thoroughly; both the likelihood of that and the impact of this objective. It became clear to me that the center likely would not want me returning to work there under any circumstances, and that my leverage was to appear as though I was very serious about wanting to return to work in the near future. In the event that I was successfully able to present this image to them, the center might be more likely to offer me a good financial settlement to ensure that I never returned.

Eventually I got back in contact with Lakisha and she informed me that the mediation was scheduled for Thursday, February 24, 2011 at 9 a.m. Interestingly, this date was exactly seven months to the day after I had first received word, on July 24, that the union would be moving my grievance onto arbitration. I told Lakisha that I was indeed interested in returning to work at the center. In reality, I was most interested in seeing the center transformed into the kind of environment that it was originally designed to be, a valuable community resource for struggling parents to utilize in order to *prevent* child abuse and neglect. It was designed to be a safe haven and last resort for our society's most vulnerable children; not a place where hostility, intimidation and corruption could openly thrive.

Around the same time that the mediation related developments were unfolding, my lawyer had recently been contacted by my case investigator at the DHR. Once again, the DHR was the state agency that was dealing with my claims of gender discrimination and retaliation. The investigator was ready to conduct an over the phone interview with me concerning my claims; this was a positive sign that the investigation was possibly nearing its end.

So on Thursday, February 10, 2011, my lawyer and I had an hour long phone conversation with the DHR investigator. It felt like the interview went great. The investigator seemed very interested in my information and impressed at my recollection of past dates and events. During our call I went over the entire case with the investigator, easily answering all of her specific inquiries. She seemed quite interested in the fact that Candy Rollins and Claudia Cahill both left the organization shortly after my wrongful termination. Along with relaying some specific incidents of discrimination; I especially placed focus on how my termination of February 1 came within exactly one week of my submitting a lengthy letter to Manager Candy Rollins on January 25, once again describing what I believed, in good faith, to be unlawful gender discrimination occurring toward me at the workplace. After all, even the center could not deny the fact that I was indeed fired exactly one week to the day after reporting discrimination to them.

I also focused on the subject matter in the letter of January 25 submitted to Candy; that being my complaints about the bathing issue created by Hilda and the negative comments about men made by her pal Samantha Jackson. As a result of the fresh info that I provided, the investigator said she would be interviewing new witnesses as well as re-interviewing some of the ones she had talked with already. She said the investigation would likely take several more weeks to complete, and that I should inform her of any new information or developments that might occur.

However, I never expected that I would get the chance to do so a mere one week after this interview. But on Thursday, February 17, 2011; my union representative, Lakisha Williams, gave me a new piece of information that all but blew me away. Once again it had to do with the conduct of one Claudia Cahill, my absolute favorite person in the world during this entire ordeal!!

Seriously speaking however, Lakisha surprisingly began to ask me questions during our mediation preparation about a website I had maintained in previous years having to do with my mental illness of Obsessive-Compulsive Disorder (OCD). On the website, I had proceeded to briefly explain the numerous different forms of OCD. Some of the info included how folks like me with this illness can experience obsessive bad thoughts and irrational fears about acting out violently; something which the OCD sufferer like me would never actually do. There is plenty of literature available about the nature of obsessive bad thoughts; and how those like me who are tormented by them are, ironically, the least likely persons within society to ever actually lose control and/or act out violently.

However according to what my union representative disclosed to me on February 17; the center's former HR Director, Claudia Cahill; had earlier come across my OCD website while searching my name on Google. Having read my posted comments, Claudia then apparently informed the union of the existence of my website and further alleged that I had printed threatening dialogue which rendered me unfit to be a child care provider! This information seemed consistent with how Claudia had repeatedly stated her belief, at the time of my termination and afterward, that she felt I posed a serious physical threat to the safety of the children. Aside from Claudia's distorted personal viewpoint, there was no evidence or documentation whatsoever to support the notion that I allegedly posed any kind of threat to the children or to anyone else. Nonetheless Claudia used this bizarre argument, fixated on her ignorant views about my mental illness, to try to persuade the employee union to not move forward with my grievance or fight to reclaim my job.

My lawyer had a lengthy chat with my DHR investigator about this. The investigator seemed very interested in this info and eager to speak with Lakisha about it. He said the investigator would soon send him paperwork to amend my original charge with the addition of perceived disability discrimination. As you may recall from chapter nine, 'physical or mental disability' is a protected class status under the Human Rights Act; just as race, gender, age, and sexual orientation are. Therefore Lakisha's disclosure that Claudia had used info concerning my mental illness against me, particularly in evaluating my capability to perform my job duties, was sufficient for me to make a new claim of perceived disability discrimination.

But while the new DHR claim was in the works, I still had to prepare for mediation. In doing so, Lakisha requested that I send her an email before February 24, explaining in precise detail what I planned to seek as a fair resolution. At long last, the moment had finally come where I would get to have my own say...

Chapter Sixteen

THE BIG MEDIATION SHOWDOWN

"I don't want mediation. I want ass kicking!" **Angry, emotional statement made on George Lopez sitcom by character George Lopez, in episode where his daughter Carmen and her bullies at school would have to engage in mediation to settle their differences.**

Along with meeting with my union representatives, I had some careful planning to do with my father in order to fully answer Lakisha's question about what I would seek as a fair resolution to this legal matter. I decided that I didn't really wish to return to work at the center, as Lakisha had assured me that the climate there had not changed much over the past year following my termination. However, I knew that in order to maintain some leverage, I needed to at least appear open to the idea of reclaiming my job. But the job was merely one of several items that I needed to address in my answer.

Fortunately, my father was of tremendous assistance to me in this area. Being highly skilled and experienced in drafting business proposals, my dad was able to construct an email for Lakisha which addressed all the issues relevant to my case.

Below is the exact context of the resolution seeking email drafted by my father that I sent to Lakisha ahead of our mediation:

Background Information

- I was an exemplary employee and a true, unique asset to this organization throughout my affiliation. I volunteered more than 160 hours of my own time to the care of vulnerable children over a twelve month period, and was awarded the high honor of being named volunteer of the year for this organization. Once I then became a paid staff member, every performance review I received while employed was very positive, and I received a special dedication award specifically highlighting my "dedication to the children and always looking out for their well-being" on Aug 19th 2009, less than six months prior to my wrongful termination on Feb. 1st 2010. Though I politely asked to be given a performance review for the year 2009, the center's management declined to ever provide me with one in spite of my written request. Therefore, I was the last person who should have been fired from the job I loved as a child care provider. My termination was entirely wrongful and without any merit or just cause.

- I was one of the very few employees who was brave enough to truly live up to my moral and legal obligations as a mandated reporter. In spite of the very real and now proven risk to my own job security, I courageously reported my own immediate supervisor's mistreatment of children on at least seven different major occasions during my employment. Many other staff persons witnessed the same incidents that I wrote up involving my supervisor and later another abusive employee, but few had the courage to truly do their legal duty and continue reporting such repeated occurrences because of the very real risk to their jobs. This did not stop me, however, from putting the safety of the children first and living up to my full moral and legal duty as a mandated reporter. Instead of receiving gratitude for my many credible reports of child mistreatment, I became a victim of an aggressive

117

campaign of retaliation towards me (for my commendable whistle-blowing activities) by management in the form of inappropriate and excessive disciplinary actions. Although I filed new grievances and diligently appealed such unfair disciplines through my employee union, this retaliation ultimately resulted in my unprovoked, wrongful termination on Feb. 1st 2010, occurring with no merit or just cause whatsoever.

- In addition to retaliation through unfair discipline, I was unofficially prohibited from bathing children for much of the last month of my employment, causing female staff members to become angry towards me for their often having to bathe my assigned children. My supervisor also spread a notion among the staff members that there was allegedly a good reason as to why I was unofficially no longer being allowed to bathe children. This form of illegal retaliation also amounts to defamation of character, which can destroy my possibility of working in the child care industry in future.

- After my wrongful termination, the center tried to stop my unemployment benefits by appealing to the Unemployment Insurance Department accusing that I had committed employment misconduct. The subsequent hearing was attended by four levels of the center's management in a most vindictive manner (my lawyer commented that he had been involved with many such hearings, but he had never come across a case where more than one level of management was involved). In spite of this display of pressure from the center's management, the Unemployment Judge concluded that I had not committed any employment misconduct, and that the evidence presented clearly showed that I was wrongfully terminated over my mandated reporting and whistle-blower activities. These proceedings were held over 3 separate hearings on 3 separate dates. I had absolutely no choice but to depend on a professional lawyer to defend myself against such a scathing attack from the center's management. These prolonged legal hearings, caused by the organization's wrongfully accusing me of employment misconduct and of posing a serious physical threat to the children, resulted in great financial expense and tremendous emotional distress.

Summary of claims

My claim consists of three parts – Part A, Part B, and Part C

Part A

This part has to do with back pay. As clearly described above, I was wrongfully terminated. I loved working with children and excelled in this role. I tried to get similar jobs in this area, but no one has been willing to hire me without a solid recommendation from my previous employer, especially in this tough economy. So, it is essential for me to receive back pay for the number of months since Feb 1, 2010

Part B

This part has to do with legal fees. As I have explained above, I had no other reasonable options besides having to depend on legal assistance to defend against the center's enormous attack on my unemployment insurance. It is therefore critical that I receive reimbursement for those expenses.

Part C

Part C is about getting my job back. As I mentioned above, I have always loved my job working with the children and excelled in this area. The center has taken this opportunity away from me. However, I understand that the center might not want me back in their organization due to what has transpired. Due to the circumstances I am willing to accept that possibility, since going back to the job would likely trigger a similar series of events since the center hasn't really made any significant changes. So I am possibly willing to accept this situation, but am not able to do this without some significant compensation. In this economy it is almost impossible for me to get another job in this line of work – especially because there is absolutely no way I can count on a positive recommendation from the center's management. Therefore, it will be critical for me to re-train myself in another line of work. I have started preparing for that possibility and believe that such training will take a minimum of two years. That is why I am asking for a compensation of 2 years' salary plus benefits for this part.

In preparing this document for Lakisha, my father explained that it was essential for me to ask for a rather high financial settlement going into the mediation. He explained that while in all likelihood I would not receive the large amount I was requesting; it is still important to push for a high figure to ensure that I would eventually end up with something that I'd find satisfactory, as people typically receive significantly less in mediation/settlement discussions than what they originally ask for.

Though I felt good about the email I sent to Lakisha, I was unable to fall asleep the night before the mediation hearing. As I lay in bed that evening, I was kept awake by the sound of my heart pounding in my chest. It was impossible to relax as all the adrenalin and anticipation flowed through me. I felt like a boxer on the night before a title fight, or a football player the night before playing in the Super Bowl. I had no idea what to expect at the mediation hearing, and felt very concerned about whether my union representatives would back me 100 percent.

Finally on the morning of Thursday, February 24, 2011, the big mediation showdown was set to begin. My dad and I arrived at the Federal Mediation Conciliation Services building shortly before 9 a.m., where we met up with union representative, Lakisha Williams and one of her senior colleagues. We were soon seated in a windowless conference room and made to wait there for the next 40 minutes. Lakisha soon learned that the center's representatives were seated separately in a nearby meeting room similar to ours.

At 9:36 a.m., the mediator introduced himself and said he'd be bringing the center's representatives into our meeting room for his introductory statement. Within moments the center's Executive Director, Karen Patrick; emerged along with two unidentified persons, a young man and a young woman who I soon learned were attorneys representing the center. I was instantly angered over the fact that the center had their high priced lawyers present, while I only had my union representatives there to defend me. Although I felt tense and was shaking slightly, I made sure to look Karen Patrick right in the eyes. She failed to return direct eye contact, a common avoidance tactic used by the cowardly and the guilty.

The mediator then went on to explain that this was a voluntary meeting, and that anyone could get up and leave at any time. He also said that everyone present, including my father, would be allowed to attend the meeting. He then informed us that after the meeting had concluded, he would soon destroy and throw away all notes he had taken during the hearing.

Following these opening remarks, the mediator then began to direct specific questions to both the center's representatives and my union representatives... and then me. This created a rather tense and uncomfortable atmosphere, as Karen Patrick and the center's lawyers began to speak negatively about my minor/frivolous disciplines and alleged poor conduct while employed by the organization. Once again, it was very aggravating to have to sit and listen to their same old, tired line of unsubstantiated allegations. These consisted of the same examples they had used unsuccessfully during the unemployment benefits hearings. The only positive in this was the fact that their arguments quickly appeared weak and irrelevant even to the mediator himself. "It looks like they're coming up with some pretty flimsy stuff," the mediator told us, moments after he excused the center's representatives from our room.

Over the next several hours, the mediator went back and forth between our two meeting rooms. However, through these proceedings, it appeared as though he had begun to assist me and understood my side in this matter. It did not take long for him to establish that I had been fired, amongst other reasons, as a form of retaliation. "I think even Ray Charles could see that," the good humored mediator went on to say. As we continued to speak with him, my father and I showed the mediator the document I'd emailed to Lakisha with my financial demands. My father especially made the strong point that he was not going to stop supporting me in this legal matter until the center had been held accountable and/or I had received good financial compensation.

Slowly the process and the mediator's efforts began to pay off. The mediator appeared to be working the center hard to get to a financial offer. He was also putting some pressure on us to come closer to accepting offers made by the center.

This is not to suggest, however, that the day's events proceeded smoothly and without distress. At one point during the process the mediator scared me by indicating someone was representing that the DHR had recently returned a finding of 'No Probable Cause' in my case! However, after I stepped out and phoned my lawyer, I confirmed that the information the mediator had received was indeed incorrect. Moments later and after some tense discussions, the mediator also assured me that the info he had received was inaccurate.

In the end, it was those long pending claims before the DHR which would serve as my powerful leverage. The mediator explained to us that while the center did not have substantial money for a settlement consisting of back pay, they had a second financial resource they could tap into; so long as it addressed a discrimination related legal matter. Therefore, the mediator explained that if I was willing to waive my DHR claims, he could likely work the center into a substantial settlement agreement.

Following more bidding and negotiating with the center through the mediator, an agreement was finally reached later that same afternoon. By 3:06 p.m., the agreement had officially been signed by both sides in this matter. In ultimately agreeing to settle my dad and I calculated that the amount the mediator had eventually gotten the center to offer me, was about the same amount that I could have hoped to receive if we had gone to trial, but then I would have had some significant legal expenses in terms of contingency plan payments. Also with this settlement, we would not have to endure the trauma of a lengthy trial and the ever-present risk of so called 'rolling the dice' and potentially losing in court. One-year and twenty-three days following my wrongful termination, it seemed as though my legal ordeal had finally come to an end!

Due to the terms of such agreements, the specific details and exact amount given in the settlement must remain confidential. Even though I did not receive my requested total amount, I am glad to say that I was very happy and satisfied with the result. Our lawyer was also quite delighted for us. It was our understanding that the amount for which we settled was a considerable amount for a case of this nature that concluded while in pre-litigation.

Along with this eventual victory, several other interesting revelations came to surface on this same day. For one, I learned that contradictory to what Lakisha had told me on October 15, the costs of arbitration are actually split between the employer and the union. I also learned that surpassing mediation does not automatically guarantee that my grievance will once again be approved to proceed onto arbitration. Naturally, these insights made me feel even more at peace with my decision to settle this case. In spite of the delays and frustration, the union had come through for me.

While this dreadful ordeal appeared to have ended for us, I couldn't help but think about all the lovable little kids still staying at the center. Even a full year after losing my job as a child care provider, I still think about my good times with the children and I still miss them a whole lot. It is my profound hope that due to what I have accomplished with this considerable settlement, the center will undergo a transformation and will no longer employ and tolerate people who mistreat and 'take their rage out' on vulnerable children. It is my profound hope that they will be much more cautious about who they hire for their HR, Children's Services Manager and Supervisor positions. It is also my profound hope that they will no longer engage in unethical behaviors; such as discrimination, whistleblower retaliation and defamation of character; which are both immoral and illegal.

From this page to God's ears, these are my profound hopes. I hope I have inspired some positive change.

Chapter Seventeen

FINAL THOUGHTS, REVELATIONS AND INSIGHTS

"I firmly believe we all have a moral responsibility to stand up for our rights and to do the right thing, regardless of the final result."

Having finally reached a positive conclusion to this legal ordeal, there are many final thoughts, revelations and insights which I now feel compelled to share with you, the reader. For better or worse, this unique life experience has taught me a lot about how both the child care system and the employment legal system work in our country.

In regard to both systems, I am sorry to say that I am profoundly disappointed with what I have learned. My greatest disappointment is directed, first and foremost, toward the child care system. To this day, I cannot understand how the DHS was unable to find both Hilda Hullickson and Crystal Matthews guilty of committing child maltreatment during their employment at the center, and thereby appropriately remove them from being in a position of power over our community's most vulnerable children.

This is especially difficult to comprehend for me, based upon all of the incredibly detailed, highly accurate documentation and up to date eyewitness contact information that I single-handedly provided to the DHS. In addition to my two hour face-to-face interview with DHS investigators in December 2009, my highly respected colleague Mary Monahan also spoke with a DHS investigator at length in February 2010. Yet I know that as of July 2010, Hilda and Crystal were *both* still employed at the center and had both been recently observed acting 'rageful' toward small children.

To this day, I remain unaware as to whether the DHS actually contacted and interviewed all of the many eyewitnesses to the long-term maltreatment of children at the center committed by both Hilda and Crystal. It was especially concerning to learn from the center's representatives, during the mediation hearing on February 24, 2011, that Hilda Hullickson still remained employed at the center as both a shift leader and a child care provider. This troubling discovery leads me to believe that the welfare of children is still not a top priority by the controlling agencies in our society. This certainly needs to change.

I also firmly believe that there are many changes that need to be made with our current employment legal system. After reading my book and hearing the sordid details of my case; I imagine people will widely question why the center engaged in such maltreatment and how so much negativity and disorder was able to thrive, seemingly out in the open, at this particular establishment. In fact throughout this case, I myself have questioned many times why presumably educated managers repeatedly subjected themselves to such unnecessary risks and liability. However, I do believe the answer to these questions is far more simple than complicated: NOBODY IN AUTHORITY BELIEVED FOR A MOMENT THAT AN EMPLOYEE COULD SUCCESSFULLY STAND UP TO THEM.

But WHY would the managers at the center have been of this particular opinion, one might choose to question, and what role might our employment legal system have in promoting this belief in my employer? While many of the issues from this story are unique to the center's environment, I believe too many employers take for granted that employees will not stand up for their basic rights. And perhaps even more unfortunate, is the fact that far too many employees also believe that they cannot dare to assert their basic rights with their employers! This especially rings true in today's tough economy, where nobody wants to do anything to potentially jeopardize their job security.

In reviewing my case, you can recall how so many people witnessed Hilda's mistreatment of children over many years' time, though precious few followed through with reporting such incidents. And when I was in need of witnesses for the unemployment benefits hearing, the majority of those I contacted did everything they could to not be involved in this matter. I am once again reminded of a statement commonly spoken by my coworker Julie Worley, "Remember, it is not our place to question things, to ask the question 'why' or to try and bring about change." It is this widespread belief among employees which causes so many arrogant employers to believe they are invincible; perhaps even more so than the employers' vast financial resources.

Still, one cannot disregard the tremendous role that money plays in favor of unjust employers. I have come to learn that our employment legal system, quite bluntly; was established to serve those with money, typically the employers; and to ignore those who don't have enough, typically the employees. Had it not been for the $22,000 my father spent on my case from February 2010 to February 2011, there is little chance that I could have prevailed in this matter. Had it not been for my parents' financial resources, I could not have even afforded the $7,000 it cost to hire a professional lawyer and defend myself in the three separate unemployment benefits hearings!

Without a good lawyer to effectively poke holes through the center's highly twisted version of events, I would have likely lost that critical battle against the center's management team. Had I lost the unemployment hearing (i.e., if the center management team was able to convince the judge that I was guilty of committing employment misconduct), I can all but guarantee that my employee union would not have chosen to back me and advance my grievance toward arbitration; a crucial move which eventually led to my receiving a considerable settlement.

In reality, I am darn lucky that my parents were both willing and able to assist me in this year-long legal ordeal. With the modest annual income of a child care provider, there was no way I could have afforded to effectively defend myself on my own. I'm sure the center's high level managers and high price legal team did not bank on the fact that a little guy like me could afford to stand up for my rights! Yet having a professional lawyer advising me was of incredible value throughout the entire process, from the demand letter to the DHR claims and through working with my employee union. The legal system needs some changes to level the playing field for other employees as well, particularly those who are just as worthy but do not have a family willing/able to help them.

But even as our flawed employment legal system stands today, WHAT STEPS CAN YOU TAKE TO STAND UP FOR YOUR BASIC RIGHTS AGAINST AN UNJUST EMPLOYER? Believe it or not, there are several easy steps which anyone can take to put themselves in a much more favorable position. Fortunately, these steps do not require money or any hard-to-obtain form of talent or representation. Rather they require paying close attention, remaining dedicated to protecting your rights and simply taking the time to advocate for yourself. Easy as it seems, most employees do not put in the time and effort necessary to prepare themselves for potential trouble at the workplace.

- Whenever acquiring a new job or position, I strongly advise you to read your employee handbook thoroughly from cover to cover. Though a bit time consuming, this is an easy step that anyone can take to inform themselves of their rights upon beginning employment.

- Make sure to read up on disciplinary procedures and educate yourself on what proper steps you can take should you run into problems at your workplace.

- I also recommend that you learn what other resources are available to you upon beginning your new job. For example, do you work for a company that is represented by an employee union and if so, who is your local union representative and how can you get in touch with them?

In my case I did not really open my employee handbook until being prompted to do so by my girlfriend; and I needed my mentor Connie Cooper to remind me of the existence of our employee union, which I would soon rely on heavily for ongoing support and assistance. Remember, as it turned out in my case, it was my employee union who truly made the difference in helping me prevail.

- As I've mentioned throughout this book; documentation is an easy, excellent means by which you can keep track of your treatment at the workplace and collect evidence to support your legal position.

Once again this can be time consuming, as I often found myself spending hours upon returning home from the workplace carefully documenting relevant incidents and events. Hopefully, most workplaces would appropriately address your concerns and issues long before the need comes to spend hours of your own time compiling evidence and documentation. In my case I met this challenge in a methodical and obsessive manner, as it also became an effective way to vent my frustrations and delve into my enjoyment of writing. In my case, it was my relentless documentation which ultimately convinced the DHR to draft a charge of discrimination against my employer. As you read, my charges through DHR later served as leverage during the mediation process. Once again, documentation is an important step any employee can choose to take on their own.

- Right along with documentation, I strongly advise you to be mindful of what topics you openly discuss at the workplace and amongst your coworkers.

This concept came into play in both of my two negative workplace situations; the earlier one at the hotel as well as this major one at the center. While being mindful is always a good idea, it becomes essential should you find yourself having problems at your workplace. Remember, you never really know who you can trust and who may stab you in the back to further their own personal agenda. If you are lucky there may be perhaps one individual at your workplace, such as my incredible shift leader Mary Monahan, who you can truly trust and count on as an ally in your ordeal. Even so, you must keep your guard up at all times. Remember that anything you reveal about your personal life, even to your closest workplace buddies, can potentially come back to haunt you at a later time. Be sure to not gossip or talk badly about a coworker, supervisor or manager who you may be having genuine problems with. If you have to take legal action against your employer in the future, you do not want several of your coworkers to later come forward and portray you as being a vindictive gossiper who talked about others in a negative manner behind their backs. This in itself, as you learned from my story, can serve as grounds for a manager like Claudia to twist things and depict you as being an insubordinate employee who did not get along well with others.

- Also, you must never tell any of your coworkers if you are contemplating taking legal action against your employer.

Aside from my mentor, Connie Cooper, who did not work at the center; I did not tell even my closest workplace buddies that I had filled out an EDQ in August 2009 or that I had been talking to various lawyers about possibly suing the center. It can be particularly difficult to remain silent when you spend countless hours around your coworkers and you're just dying to vent to your buddies. Believe me when I say that I know how this feels. It can be hard to resist the impulse to share opinions about a person you do not like and develop camaraderie with your coworkers who may understand and be in a similar situation. As human beings, we naturally long for validation and vindication about our feelings from our peers. But remember, the last thing in the world that you want to do is give your employer a heads up, especially if you find yourself pondering the idea of pursuing legal action! Again, being mindful in this way is an easy step which any employee can choose to take, though precious few may have the self-discipline necessary to successfully do so. Remaining cautious and silent can truly pay off in the end, both literally and figuratively.

- Also, it is important to never engage in any form of sexual joking at the workplace.

Such innocent playfulness, even among fully participating coworkers, can come back to haunt you later should you find yourself pursuing legal action in the future. As you have learned well from my story; employers can be extremely creative, twisted and outrageous in bogus claims they may level against you in an attempt to impeach your credibility. Therefore, it is your responsibility to not give them any additional material to work with.

- When in the throes of an impending legal situation; it is essential to be mindful of what information you communicate to others in the form of emails, text messages, Facebook postings, Tweets, letters, voicemail messages and any other forms of communication that can later be traced back to you.

131

In my case it was clear to see how the center's high priced lawyer attempted to use the email against me, during unemployment benefits hearings, that I had sent to the center's former receptionist in which I described Claudia Cahill in far less than flattering terms. Even in sharing genuine frustration and venting with supporters and loved ones, try not to say anything in writing that can later be twisted by your employer and used against you. This will require some vigilance and self-discipline on your part. Remember, an employer will do absolutely anything they can think up to discredit you if you're taking legal action against them!

- If you are being harassed or observing misconduct at your workplace, it is important to disclose all such incidents to your employer in a manner that is appropriate and in accordance with following the proper chain of command.

Many employees feel it is too risky to report inappropriate conduct involving their superiors to higher authorities, as was the case with many of my coworkers at the center. However, I firmly believe that officially disclosing your concerns in good faith is essential to protecting your rights in the long run and potentially building a case against your employer. After all, how was the unemployment law judge in my case able to correctly determine, over the telephone mind you, that I had been fired as a form of retaliation for my whistle-blowing activities? It is because there was a long line of documented concerns made by me to management, to the board of directors and to my employee union; all leading up to my wrongful termination. With a documented history of reported concerns, it becomes easier for the DHR or a judge or a lawyer to see how you were indeed a victim of retaliation. Once this pattern can be clearly established, the likelihood of prevailing and/or receiving a settlement naturally increases for you.

Along these lines, it is essential for you to disclose misconduct to your employer that may be either discriminatory and/or sexually offensive in nature. Remember, employers are not to punish or terminate you in response to your disclosing what you honestly perceive, in good faith, to be unlawful discrimination or sexual harassment occurring at the workplace. There are legal consequences for such improper actions. Even if the negative conduct you alleged is later found to have not actually consisted of discrimination and/or sexual harassment, it is still illegal for your employer to wrongfully punish or terminate you for disclosing your potential concerns of this nature. I believe this played a major role in my DHR claims against my employer. After all, nobody can dispute the fact that I was indeed fired exactly one week after I disclosed what I still believed to be gender discrimination toward me by both Hilda and Samantha Jackson. Had the center not wisely opted to settle with me during mediation, I am confident that the DHR would have found 'probable cause' at least in the form of retaliation for my disclosing perceived discrimination to my employer. Obviously, the center had realized that at some point in this process.

- When speaking with a legal authority who is investigating various aspects of your case during a legal ordeal; whether it be a judge, a human rights investigator, a mediator, etc.; make sure to keep your emotions firmly in check and do not become angry, defensive or assume they are turning against you if they direct challenging questions your way.

In my case I experienced a moment of this nature during my unemployment benefits hearing on Friday, July 9, 2010. Had I panicked and reacted with anger or defensiveness in response to the judge's challenging question; I might then have turned the judge off and, ironically, persuaded him to rule against me. Instead, I remained cool and calm and sincerely explained my position to "Your Honor." As it turned out, the judge believed me in the end. It is important to note that I also experienced such 'challenging questions' from my DHR investigator on February 10,

2011; as well as from the mediator on February 24, 2011. Fortunately, I handled these in a similar positive manner. As you have read it paid off. Therefore, it is very important for an individual to stay calm and keep their emotions in check whenever being questioned by an authority figure in regard to a legal ordeal. Believe it or not, this could literally make all the difference between either winning or losing in a case!

•   In a legal ordeal, it is important that you do not allow yourself to become discouraged and/or distressed due to the length of time the matter may take to resolve.

In my case, you can recall how frustrated and stressed I felt many times as this legal matter very slowly progressed. In truth, there were many unhappy times when my family and I could not relax. There were so many days when I had no idea whether any progress was being made in my case, and felt as though I had no control over what the outcome would be. This frustration and helplessness was only intensified when I would frequently be unable to establish contact and communication with my union representative. In the end I spent about a year and a half waiting. First, from August 2009 to January 2010, for the DHR to draft a charge, during which time I continued to suffer at work; then get to a near final determination. Then I spent the remaining year, February 2010 to February 2011, waiting for my employee union to very gradually move my grievance toward arbitration. Even after being awarded a settlement during mediation on February 24, the following three months were spent negotiating the terms of that agreement with the center's attorneys, all of which had to be done before I could get my hands on the check.

Naturally, unjust employers try their best to delay legal proceedings for as long as possible, in hopes that the employee will not have either the money or emotional patience to wait-it-out and still win in the end. Therefore, it is essential to not allow frustration and stress to affect your closest relationships or your resolve to succeed. How you deal with your negative emotions is within your own control, unlike many other aspects of the unpredictable legal process. Remember, your unjust employer is counting on you to self-destruct and simply let them off the hook, like countless others before you have done. Your perseverance can indeed make a difference in this regard. Like Hannah Montana says in her popular song lyrics, it's all about the 'climb' and you must not give up!

•   When considering a job in a certain workplace environment where you may stand out as being different for any reason, it may help to be mentally prepared to potentially encounter some forms of discrimination.

In sharing this sensitive piece of advice, it is not at all my intention to discourage you from following your dreams and pursuing the line of work that you wish to choose for yourself. However at the same time, I feel some mental preparation and awareness could be a positive thing for you in the long-run, especially in regards to understanding your rights and keeping tabs on the manner in which you are being treated. In my case, I never thought twice about the fact that I would be a minority as a male working in the child care industry. In volunteering and working at the center, I was initially welcomed with open arms for entering an environment where members of the male gender were extremely hard to come by. Unfortunately with the passage of time in my case, I began to experience differential treatment clearly based upon my gender as a male, and also possibly based upon my ethnicity. Though I do not plan to let this difficult experience influence my future employment choices, it helps me now to be aware of the possible discrimination issues which can result from being a minority at any workplace.

Unfortunately, even following these several, well thought out steps does not guarantee you will prevail in the final outcome of a legal ordeal. There is often luck and numerous other factors involved which we simply cannot control. Still, I firmly believe we all have a moral responsibility to stand up for our rights and to do the right thing, regardless of the final result. I firmly believe that the more we choose to stand up and fight for what's right in this life, the better our chances become of eventually overcoming the greater injustice.

Please know that I wish you the best of luck in any future legal event. Although I am not a lawyer, I sincerely hope that you can benefit from my personal experiences and reflections I have provided in this book. If ever faced with such a trying ordeal, I sincerely hope you can get to the point with your unjust employer where I was finally able to get with the center... where all they could do in the end was to desperately beg, "Hey, don't sue me... Sumi!"

###

About the Author

Author and Speaker Sumi Mukherjee writes non-fiction books based on real life stories and speaks to audiences about the messages contained in his books. His focus is on bringing about positive changes in our society, with specific emphasis on prevention of bullying and child sexual abuse. Since October 2011, Sumi has been speaking to hundreds of people around the country so others can benefit from his stories. Sumi has spoken to teachers, counselors, administrators, social workers, school psychologists, mental health professionals, family members, caregivers, service providers, law enforcement professionals, students, parents and the general audience. He has spoken at schools, colleges, religious organizations, bullying prevention conferences, other professional conferences; including School Social Workers Association conferences, School Psychologists Association Conference, Counseling Association Conferences and State Psychological Association Conferences; child abuse prevention conferences, domestic violence/sexual abuse/mental health awareness events. Sumi has spoken extensively all over the United States as well as in Canada. Sumi was born in Calgary, Canada, and grew up in Minneapolis, USA. For more information please visit his website at www.authorsumi.com

Made in the USA
Middletown, DE
28 January 2017